Neo4j Graph Data Modeling

Design efficient and flexible databases by optimizing the power of Neo4j

Mahesh Lal

PUBLISHING

BIRMINGHAM - MUMBAI

Neo4j Graph Data Modeling

First published: July 2015

Production reference: 1230715

Published by Packt Publishing Ltd.
Livery Place
35 Livery Street
Birmingham B3 2PB, UK.

ISBN 978-1-78439-344-1

www.packtpub.com

Credits

Author
Mahesh Lal

Reviewers
Patrick Baumgartner

Sonal Raj

Daniel Vaughan

Acquisition Editor
Shaon Basu

Content Development Editor
Kirti Patil

Technical Editor
Mrunmayee Patil

Copy Editor
Pranjali Chury

Project Coordinator
Nidhi Joshi

Proofreader
Safis Editing

Indexer
Mariammal Chettiyar

Production Coordinator
Conidon Miranda

Cover Work
Conidon Miranda

About the Author

Mahesh Lal is a developer who has experience with various technologies. In 2011, while working on a social network for a client, he discovered the power of graphs, specifically Neo4j. Since then, he has been working with multiple clients across various domains for modeling their data as a graph. Currently working for ThoughtWorks, India, he is trying to help his clients look at their search problems in the form of a graph.

I would like to thank my reviewers, Daniel Vaughan, Sonal Raj, and Patrick Baumgartner, for giving me valuable feedback. I am grateful to Jim Webber and Pramod Sadalge for guiding me through this journey. I am indebted to my colleagues at ThoughtWorks for believing in me. Finally, I'd like to thank my family, who always inspire me to improve.

About the Reviewers

Patrick Baumgartner works as a passionate software craftsman at 42talents and builds software with Java/JEE, Spring Framework, OSGi, NoSQL databases, and other open source technologies. Since he began working with Neo4j in 2010, he sees the whole world as one big connected graph.

He is the host of the Neo4j Zurich and the Software Craftsmanship Zurich Meetup group and is actively involved in the agile community in Switzerland.

As a Spring trainer and Neo4j master instructor, he conducts various training and workshops on the topic, is an active speaker at conferences and events, and lectures at technical colleges. In his free time, he likes to explore Rik's Beer Graph or his own Single Malt Whisky Graph and tries to find routes to beautiful places.

Patrick has coauthored the German book, *OSGi für Praktiker*, with Bernd Weber and Oliver Braun and reviewed *Scala - Objektfunktionale Programmierung* by Oliver Braun.

I would like to thank my dearest girlfriend, Carmen, for supporting me in all my adventures.

Sonal Raj is a hacker, Pythonista, big data believer, and a technology dreamer. He has a passion for design and is an artist at heart. He blogs about technology, design, and gadgets at `http://www.sonalraj.com/`. When not working on projects, he can be found travelling, stargazing, or reading.

He has pursued engineering in computer science and loves to work on community projects. He has been a research fellow at IISc Bangalore and has taken up projects on graph computations using Neo4j and Storm. Sonal has been a speaker at PyCon India and local meetups about Neo4j, and has also published articles and research papers for leading magazines and international journals. He has contributed to several open source projects. Presently, Sonal works at Goldman Sachs.

He is the author of *Neo4j High Performance* and has reviewed titles on Storm and Neo4j.

I am grateful to the author for patiently listening to my critiques, and I'd like to thank the open source community for keeping their passions alive and contributing to such remarkable projects. A special thank you to my parents, without whom I never would have grown to love learning as much as I do.

Daniel Vaughan has worked as a software developer for over 15 years and is still learning every day. He first started using Neo4j in 2010, and currently works for the European Bioinformatics Institute, Hinxton, Cambridge, UK. He is married to Michelle and lives in the quaint market town of Saffron Walden.

Daniel has previously authored *Ext GWT 2.0, Beginner's Guide* and worked on the *Spring Web Services 2, Cookbook*, both by Packt Publishing.

His website is `http://www.danielvaughan.com` and you can find him on Twitter at `@DanielVaughan`.

www.PacktPub.com

Support files, eBooks, discount offers, and more

For support files and downloads related to your book, please visit www.PacktPub.com.

Did you know that Packt offers eBook versions of every book published, with PDF and ePub files available? You can upgrade to the eBook version at www.PacktPub.com and as a print book customer, you are entitled to a discount on the eBook copy. Get in touch with us at service@packtpub.com for more details.

At www.PacktPub.com, you can also read a collection of free technical articles, sign up for a range of free newsletters and receive exclusive discounts and offers on Packt books and eBooks.

https://www2.packtpub.com/books/subscription/packtlib

Do you need instant solutions to your IT questions? PacktLib is Packt's online digital book library. Here, you can search, access, and read Packt's entire library of books.

Why subscribe?

- Fully searchable across every book published by Packt
- Copy and paste, print, and bookmark content
- On demand and accessible via a web browser

Free access for Packt account holders

If you have an account with Packt at www.PacktPub.com, you can use this to access PacktLib today and view 9 entirely free books. Simply use your login credentials for immediate access.

To my family, who inspire me to shed fear, reach high, and be sure.

Table of Contents

Preface

Graph databases have been gaining traction for a long time now and companies have adopted them for various use cases. Neo4j, the world's leading graph database, has been at the forefront of this trend and is widely used in production by companies that are world leaders in their respective domains. Advice on the usage of Neo4j using Cypher (the Neo4j query language), performance tuning of Neo4j, and general information can be sourced from various sources, including, but not limited to, blogs, the Neo4j website, the Neo4j mailing list, as well as books written by authors on these subjects. However, there is limited information regarding modeling information in Neo4j. This book aims to address this gap by giving examples of how various scenarios can be modeled in Neo4j. By sticking to a nonsocial graph example, this book steers clear of the stereotypical use case of graph databases. While we use Neo4j as an example to discuss graph database modeling, the concepts discussed can be applied to any graph database. We believe this book to be a useful tool for anyone wishing to understand graph database modeling.

What this book covers

Chapter 1, Graphs Are Everywhere, introduces you to the logical data representation of a property graph model, the various use cases of graph databases, and the advantages of using graph databases in general and Neo4j in particular.

Chapter 2, Modeling Flights and Cities, introduces you to basic modeling in Neo4j by discussing how flights and cities can be modeled in a graph database. We then create cities and flights in Neo4j using Cypher.

Chapter 3, Formulating an Itinerary, discusses some basic querying using Cypher for the purpose of creating a light itinerary from the existing data in Neo4j.

Chapter 4, Modeling Bookings and Users, discusses how to represent, in a graph database, a data model that is traditionally implemented in a RDBMS by modeling bookings in Neo4j.

Chapter 5, Refactoring the Data Model, covers refactoring the data model to accommodate changes in the business using Cypher. We do this as a multistep process and demonstrate how simple it is in Neo4j to change the data model.

Chapter 6, Modeling Communication Chains, discusses how communication chains can be modeled in Neo4j. This also covers how we can represent temporal relationships using this modeling technique, which allows for efficient retrieval of data while maintaining the integrity of the relationships between various pieces of information.

Chapter 7, Modeling Access Control, focuses on how access control lists can be modeled in Neo4j. This also discusses how hierarchies and groups can be modeled in Neo4j.

Chapter 8, Recommendations and Analysis of Historical Data, demonstrates the construction of queries to recommend cities and hotels to travelers using the data that we have in the database. This also analyzes some historical data to discover patterns in the database. This chapter demonstrates queries that would normally require some heavy lifting in an RDBMS.

Chapter 9, Wrapping Up, is the final chapter and talks about potential issues that you might run into while using Neo4j or a graph database, and also how modeling for a current problem isn't future-proof.

What you need for this book

To be able to learn from this book effectively, you must have Neo4j 2.2.3 (or higher) installed on your machine. Neo4j runs on Windows, Linux, and Mac OS X machines. The queries in this book have also been tested with Neo4j 2.3.0-M02.

Who this book is for

If you are a developer who wants to understand the fundamentals of modelling data in Neo4j and how it can be used to model full-fledged applications, then this book is for you. Some understanding of domain modelling may be advantageous, but is not essential.

Conventions

In this book, you will find a number of text styles that distinguish between different kinds of information. Here are some examples of these styles and an explanation of their meaning.

Code words in text, database table names, folder names, filenames, file extensions, pathnames, dummy URLs, user input, and Twitter handles are shown as follows: "The MATCH clause is used to match a path having the specified node and relationship types."

A block of code is set as follows:

```
neo4j-sh (?)$ CREATE CONSTRAINT ON (user:User) ASSERT
  user.email IS UNIQUE;
```

New terms and **important words** are shown in bold like this: "A city can have multiple categories and will be connected to all categories that it has by a **:KNOWN_ FOR** relationship."

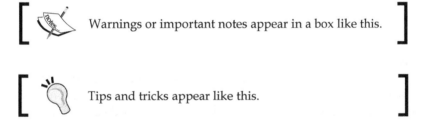

> Warnings or important notes appear in a box like this.

> Tips and tricks appear like this.

Reader feedback

Feedback from our readers is always welcome. Let us know what you think about this book—what you liked or disliked. Reader feedback is important for us as it helps us develop titles that you will really get the most out of.

To send us general feedback, simply e-mail feedback@packtpub.com, and mention the book's title in the subject of your message.

If there is a topic that you have expertise in and you are interested in either writing or contributing to a book, see our author guide at www.packtpub.com/authors.

Customer support

Now that you are the proud owner of a Packt book, we have a number of things to help you to get the most from your purchase.

Downloading the example code

You can download the example code files from your account at http://www. packtpub.com for all the Packt Publishing books you have purchased. If you purchased this book elsewhere, you can visit http://www.packtpub.com/support and register to have the files e-mailed directly to you.

Downloading the color images of this book

We also provide you with a PDF file that has color images of the screenshots/ diagrams used in this book. The color images will help you better understand the changes in the output. You can download this file from https://www.packtpub. com/sites/default/files/downloads/3441OS_ColoredImages.pdf.

Errata

Although we have taken every care to ensure the accuracy of our content, mistakes do happen. If you find a mistake in one of our books—maybe a mistake in the text or the code—we would be grateful if you could report this to us. By doing so, you can save other readers from frustration and help us improve subsequent versions of this book. If you find any errata, please report them by visiting http://www.packtpub. com/submit-errata, selecting your book, clicking on the **Errata Submission Form** link, and entering the details of your errata. Once your errata are verified, your submission will be accepted and the errata will be uploaded to our website or added to any list of existing errata under the Errata section of that title.

To view the previously submitted errata, go to https://www.packtpub.com/books/ content/support and enter the name of the book in the search field. The required information will appear under the **Errata** section.

Piracy

Piracy of copyrighted material on the Internet is an ongoing problem across all media. At Packt, we take the protection of our copyright and licenses very seriously. If you come across any illegal copies of our works in any form on the Internet, please provide us with the location address or website name immediately so that we can pursue a remedy.

Please contact us at copyright@packtpub.com with a link to the suspected pirated material.

We appreciate your help in protecting our authors and our ability to bring you valuable content.

eBooks, discount offers, and more

Did you know that Packt offers eBook versions of every book published, with PDF and ePub files available? You can upgrade to the eBook version at www.PacktPub.com and as a print book customer, you are entitled to a discount on the eBook copy. Get in touch with us at customercare@packtpub.com for more details.

At www.PacktPub.com, you can also read a collection of free technical articles, sign up for a range of free newsletters, and receive exclusive discounts and offers on Packt books and eBooks.

Questions

If you have a problem with any aspect of this book, you can contact us at questions@packtpub.com, and we will do our best to address the problem.

1

Graphs Are Everywhere

Graphs are all around us. Each time we access the Internet, the data packets travel across a network of routers, switches, and cables and deliver what we have requested. While representing key concepts/objects in a problem and defining relationships or interactions between the concepts/objects involved, we generally draw bubbles or boxes to denote the objects, and arrows between those objects to represent the interactions or relationships. We use a similar notation while drawing a map to explain routes to others. The beauty of these notations, such as bubbles and arrows, is their expressiveness, a property that is usually lost when we obfuscate the model into records and tables. Graphs allow us to discover information and ease the modeling pain, which eventually makes our life smoother. To be able to use graphs better, we will need to understand a few basic concepts related to a graph database. In this chapter, we will explore the following:

- Graphs in mathematics
- The property graph model
- Reasons for using a graph database
- Usage of graphs — some obvious and some not-so-obvious graph problems
- Advantages of using Neo4j

We chose **Neo4j** to explain graph data modeling in this book. However, the modeling concepts discussed here will apply to any graph database.

A few readers might be experienced Neo4j users and if you fall into this category, you might want to skip this chapter. However, if you are new to Neo4j or want a brief refresher, please carry on.

Graphs in mathematics

A graph is a mathematical structure of objects in which some pairs of objects are connected by links. The objects are denoted by abstractions called **nodes** (also known as **vertices**) and their links are represented by relationships (also known as **edges**). The relationships might be directed where it makes semantic sense in one particular direction. In cases where the semantics work in both directions, we can safely use undirected relationships to denote the link.

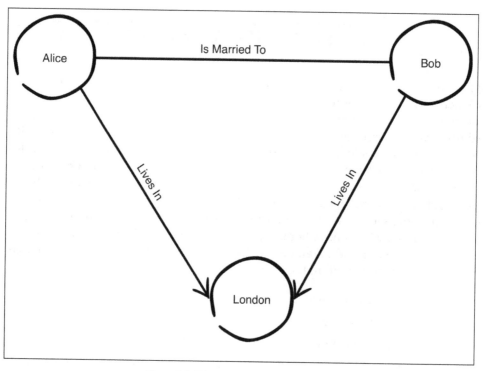

Figure 1.1: Edges, vertices, directionality

In *Figure 1.1*, we have three actors or entities, **Alice**, **Bob**, and **London**, which are represented as nodes. The links between them are denoted by relationships. Alice is married to Bob and Bob is married to Alice. Both true, hence we represent **Is Married To** as an **undirected** relationship. However, Alice lives in London is represented by a directed relationship, **Lives In**, from **Alice** to **London**. This is because London lives in Alice cannot be true.

The property graph model

In Neo4j, we use a property graph model to represent information. The property graph model is an extension of the graphs from mathematics. The following figure gives an example of how data from *Figure 1.1* can be represented in Neo4j:

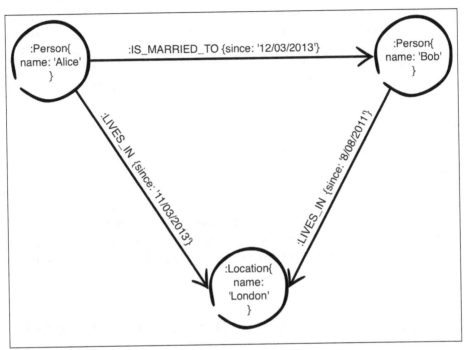

Figure 1.2: Nodes, relationships and properties

The preceding figure introduces the following concepts that we use to model a property graph:

- **Nodes**: Entities are modelled as nodes. In *Figure 1.2*, **London, Bob, Alice** are all entities.

- **Labels**: These are used to represent the role of the node in our domain. A node can have multiple labels at the same time. Apart from adding more meaning to nodes, labels are also used to add constraints and indices that are local to the particular label. In the preceding figure, **:Person** and **:Location** are the two labels that we used. We can add an index or constraint on **name** for each of these labels, which will result in two separate indices—one for **:Location** and the other for **:Person**.

- **Relationships**: These depict directed, semantically relevant connections between two nodes. A relationship in Neo4j will always have a start node, an end node, and a single type. While relationships need to be created with a direction, we can ignore the direction while traversing them. **:LIVES_IN** and **:IS_MARRIED_TO** in *Figure 1.2* are relationship types.

- **Properties**: These are key-value pairs that contain information about the node or relationship. In the previous figure, **name** and **since** are both properties that divulge more information about the node or relationship they are associated with. Neo4j can accept any **Java Virtual Machine (JVM)** type as a property, including but not limited to, date, string, double, and arrays.

This property graph model allows us to model data as close to the real world as possible.

The resultant model is simpler and more expressive. It also explicitly calls out relationships. In contrast to an RDBMS, which uses foreign keys to imply relationships, having them explicitly defined allows us to retrieve data by traversing relationships to find the information we need. This is a deliberate, practical algorithmic approach that uses the connectedness of data, rather than relying on some index lookups or joins to find the related data. Explicit relationships also make the property graph model a natural fit for most problem domains, as they are interconnected.

Storage – native graph storage versus non-native graph storage

As with all database management systems, graph databases have the concept of storage and query engines, which deal with persistence and queries over connected data. The query engine of the database is responsible for running the queries and retrieving or modifying data. The query engine exposes the graph data model through Create, Read, Update, and Delete operations (commonly referred to as CRUD). Storage deals with how the data is stored physically and how it is represented logically when retrieved. Its knowledge can help in choosing a graph database.

Relationships are an important part of any domain model and need to be traversed frequently. In a graph database, the relationships are explicit rather than inferred. Making relationships explicit is achieved either via the query engine working on a non-native graph storage (such as RDBMS, column stores, document stores) or using a native graph storage.

In a graph database relying on non-native graph storage, relationships need to be inferred at runtime. For example, if we want to model a graph in an RDBMS, our processing engine will have to infer the relationships using foreign keys and reify the relationships at runtime. This problem is computationally expensive and is infeasible for traversing multiple relationships because of the recursive joins involved. There are other graph databases in which NoSQL stores such as HDFS, column stores such as Cassandra, or documents are used to store data and expose a Graph API. Though there are no joins in a graph database using NoSQL stores, the database still has to use index lookups. In cases where non-native storage is used, the query engines have to make more computational effort.

Neo4j uses a native graph storage. Each node has a handle to all the outgoing relationships it has and each relationship, in turn, knows its terminal nodes. At runtime, to find neighboring nodes, Neo4j doesn't have to do an index lookup. Instead, neighboring nodes can be identified by looking at the relationships of the current node. This feature is called **index-free adjacency**. Index-free adjacency is mechanically sympathetic and allows the Neo4j query engine to have a significant performance boost while traversing the graph.

Reasons to use graph databases

Every morning when we check our Facebook feed, we are welcomed by a stream of updates from friends and news. Using information about how data is connected and matching it with our individual preferences, Facebook builds a stream of activities from our network that are relevant and interest us. LinkedIn does something similar while suggesting jobs within our network. When we fire up Google Maps or some application such as TomTom or Sygic maps and start navigating to a destination, we use the data that represents connections of various intersections within the city, and work out how best to traverse it. While shopping online, products are recommended to us based on how closely they are connected to what we have already bought or similar products that others have bought. We leverage connected data more and more every day without realizing it.

When dealing with connected data, a graph database gives us the following advantages:

- The query performance of a graph database is a few orders of magnitude better than RDBMS or other NoSQL alternatives. As the dataset grows, RDBMS join performance deteriorates because of the ever-increasing size of the join tables. On the other hand, graph traversals are localized to a portion of the graph. So query execution time is proportional to the number of nodes visited, rather than being proportional to the overall amount of data stored. This makes the query performance fairly constant over time even though the data might increase exponentially.

- Flexibility and agility are major considerations in today's world where business needs are constantly evolving. Developers need to have a tool that allows them to incrementally think of the model rather than locking down the data model before they start coding. Graph databases allow for addition of relationships, node types, and properties without making any changes to the existing queries. We can connect the model incrementally, thereby allowing for more sophisticated querying. This flexibility also means fewer migrations. Even in case of changes to the data model, migrations are relatively pain free and can be done without taking the database offline for a long time, thus helping teams deliver software faster while concentrating on the domain rather than managing infrastructure and communication.

- Lesser ambiguity leads to better models. Since graph databases are schema-less, the schema is dictated by the application and hence is better validated. It allows for better design thinking by developers since there is no ambiguity of the domain model compared to how it is stored in tables.

- The design to delivery time is reduced. From a developer's standpoint, one of the best features of a graph database is that it is whiteboard friendly. We can make a data model on a whiteboard and not worry about trying to translate it to a set of tables, which don't necessarily represent the data model as is. This allows the developers to concentrate on development rather than translation, thereby saving time.

While all that has been said might seem like jargon, it boils down to economics. Graph databases make more economic sense when the data is highly connected.

What to use a graph database for

Let's start by citing a few problem statements that are more suited to graph databases.

Routing is a graph problem and much research has been done in that respect. One of the leading delivery services in the world uses a Neo4j-based solution to route packages in real time based on information being collected worldwide.

Social networks are problems suited for graphs since they leverage the connections of users to fetch data and decide on what is accessible and what isn't. Facebook, in particular, uses its graph search and has exposed it to the users to enable them to make better searches. Facebook relies heavily on the graph of people and their friends to curate the feed.

Recommendation is again a graph problem that can be solved using graph databases. While companies such as eBay originally relied on MySQL, they eventually turned to Neo4j.

While routing, social networks and recommendations are all obvious graph problems, companies have solved a host of problems by fitting the data into graphs in the recent past.

Search, for example, doesn't come across as a graph problem and is not a very intuitive one. However, Google uses its Knowledge Graph to give you search results based on how well connected a piece of content is to the term being searched. More recently, Facebook has leveraged its social graph to help search become better.

Medical research is another domain where graphs are being used. Medical data is highly interconnected and hence can benefit greatly from the use of graph databases. Companies are now using graph databases for drug discovery and storing medical information.

Storage of ontologies is increasingly being solved using graph databases, which are rapidly finding applications in machine learning and analytics. Companies are also using graph databases in domains such as energy supply and transportation.

Choosing Neo4j for exploring graph databases

Neo4j is a fast, native graph database that satisfies **Atomicity, Consistency, Isolation, Durability (ACID)** properties. Through usage of transactions, developers can ensure that the failure of a transaction leaves the database's state unchanged ensuring atomicity. Any change to the database doesn't destroy data, ensuring consistency. Data modified by a transaction is isolated from other transactions till it is committed. Since Neo4j is a persistent graph database, the results of a committed transaction can always be retrieved, thus making it durable.

It started off supporting the **TinkerPop** stack. More information about the TinkerPop stack can be found at `http://www.tinkerpop.com`.

Neo4j provides numerous modeling and technical affordances, which are valuable when building real-world systems such as:

- Neo4j is the most mature graph database and has been in production round the clock since 2003. Neo4j is open source with an enormous community. The Neo4j development team is highly engaged with that community so that the features and bugs are rapidly addressed. Neo4j provides native graph storage that enables its engine to perform native graph processing. From the query language to disks, everything is mechanically sympathetic to the transactional storage and rapid retrieval of graph data.

- Cypher is a very expressive query language used to retrieve data from Neo4j. While it is superficially similar to SQL in some respect, Cypher is the only declarative query language that is built ground-up for humane yet performant graph queries and writes. The Neo4j Java API can be used on JVM-based languages as a more imperative and performant method of querying. This gives the best of both worlds by supporting imperative and declarative querying. (Neo4j plans to move away from supporting Gremlin in the long run, and currently Gremlin is supported through a plugin). Neo4j is open source and allows plugins to enhance or add functionalities, and there is a vibrant ecosystem of tooling around the core database.

- Any Cypher statement that updates the graph is run within a transaction. If a transaction exists, the newly fired Cypher query will be run in it. If no transaction exists, then the statement will itself be transactional.

- The community being fostered is incredible. This is also partly made possible by the project being open source. Neo4j is currently being used in production by companies such as UBS, Cisco, Walmart, eBay, Telenor, HP, Pitney Bowes, Accenture, Lockheed Martin, Glassdoor, and many others.

The structure of the book

This book is divided into two sections:

- Section 1 (*Chapter 2*, *Modeling Flights and Cities*, to *Chapter 5*, *Refactoring the Data Model*) is essential to understand graph modeling concepts that you will use in your daily routine. We cover how to model a graph, how to query it, how to evolve a graph database to accommodate changes in the domain, and how to translate a RDBMS data model into a graph design.

- Section 2 (*Chapter 6*, *Modeling Communication Chains*, to *Chapter 8*, *Recommendations and Analysis of Historical Data*) are more reference oriented with models that you might need for optimization or for specialized cases. Topics covered are modeling chains and advantages of modeling chains, modeling access control, and designing recommendation systems based on the data present.

Summary

In this chapter, we discussed that graph databases are structures that help represent data as nodes, relationships, and properties; relationships explicitly specify and qualify the connection between two entities; labels add semantic meaning to nodes and allow for addition of indices and constraints; properties add more information to the nodes and relationships. We saw a few use cases in which graphs are used currently.

From the next chapter onward, we will delve into designing a data model and use actual Cypher queries to feed it into Neo4j. The queries used in this book are compatible with Neo4j 2.2.3. They have also been tested with Neo4j 2.3.0-M02.

2
Modeling Flights and Cities

We looked at what graphs are and what domains they might be suited for. Now, it is time to dive deeper into concepts that are related to graph databases and how we can go ahead and create our data in a graph. In this chapter, we will look at:

- How graphs can be used outside the social context modeling flights and cities for creating an itinerary
- Adding nodes, labels, properties, relationships, uniqueness constraints, and indices

Before we dive deep into modeling, we recommend that you download the code samples that you will need to run the examples in this chapter. The code can be downloaded from `https://github.com/maheshlal2910/neo4j_graph_data_modelling`.

Graphs are more than social

Often, when we talk about graph databases and their most suited use cases, people point out that social networks are a good use case for graphs. While this is true, in a way, it pigeonholes graph databases. Graph databases are versatile tools that can be used to model various domains and problems. In this book, we pick up a nonsocial example — travel, and explain how we can model data for various subsystems that would be used in a travel website using Neo4j.

Designing a system to get a travel itinerary

The travel domain is interesting in terms of data modeling challenges. Throughout this book, we will be modeling systems that work together in a website that can be used for planning flight travel. Travelers would like to look at the options for an itinerary before booking any particular set of flights, especially if there is no direct flight from the traveler's current city to the destination city. Normally, an itinerary includes total duration, layover duration, and the number of hops it takes to reach the destination. We cannot, however, derive the itinerary without modeling cities and flights, which brings us to our first data modeling problem.

Introduction to modeling flights and cities

If we were to explain the problem of cities and the number of flights between them, we could start with drawing cities as nodes. In case two cities have two or more direct flights between them, we connect those two cities with an undirected relationship, as shown in the following figure:

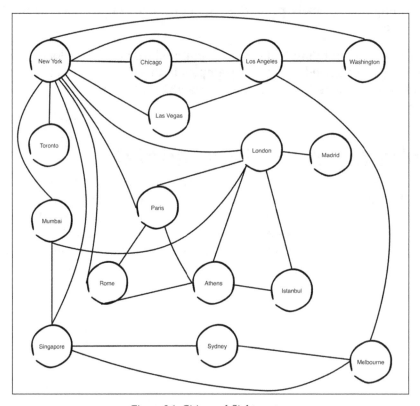

Figure 2.1: Cities and flight routes

In the situation depicted by *Figure 2.1*, there is a direct route between **New York** and the following cities: **Chicago**, **Los Angeles**, **Washington**, and **Las Vegas**, for instance. However, if a traveler has to fly to New York from Istanbul, they have to choose from among the following routes:

- Istanbul — London — New York
- Istanbul — Athens — Paris — New York

In *Figure 2.1*, an undirected relationship between cities that are connected by flights is an abstraction stating that there are at least two direct flights between those two cities. For example, between New York and Los Angeles, there should be one flight from New York to Los Angeles and vice versa. In reality, there might be multiple flights, operated by different operators, travelling to and fro between two cities that are directly connected in *Figure 2.1*. This complicates the problem of presenting the traveler with a good itinerary.

Identifying the entities

Before we jump to modeling, we need to identify the interacting entities involved in this problem. For the problem of creating an itinerary, we need cities and flights connecting them. Cities form hubs, which one can travel to or transit through. Flights fly from one city to another.

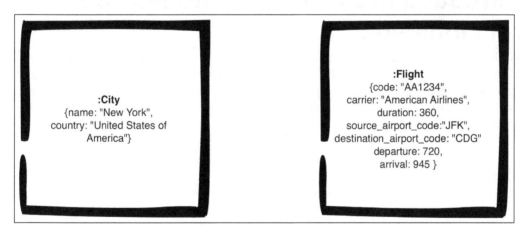

Figure 2.2: Cities and flights

The preceding figure represents the information that is needed and applicable to both the entities. While city names aren't unique in the real world, we could use city names to uniquely identify the city in our domain. In addition to the name, a city will also have the name of the country it belongs to.

A flight can be uniquely identified by its code. Other parameters include duration of the flight (in minutes), departure and arrival time (in minutes within the day where 0000 hrs will be 0 minutes and 2359 hrs will be 1439 minutes). We capture information about the airports between which the flight operates in **source_airport_ code** and **destination_airport_code**.

In the RDBMS world, an attribute that uniquely identifies a record is called a **primary key**. More often than not, this primary key attribute is denoted by prefixing pk_ to its name. Also, primary keys are mostly some sort of long integer. In this book, we will use UUIDs as primary keys wherever other attributes can't be used as primary keys. However, in cases where we can use any property as a key, we will (for convenience) use that field as a key. Please note that in production systems, the key should be a distinct property serving a single purpose — uniquely identifying the node/relationship. Also, having either long integers or UUIDs as IDs allows us to use them in URLs where other properties might not be usable.

Introduction to modeling nodes and relationships

We looked at the data models in *Figure 2.2*. Without delving into technical details, we can say that "A person can fly from New York to London on carrier X". With this statement, we can start exploring possibilities in which this data can be modelled. A preliminary approach would be to mark cities as nodes and flights as relationships, as shown in the following figure:

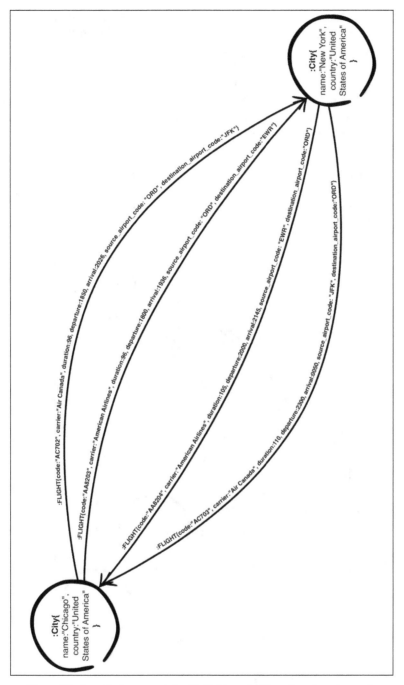

Figure 2.3: A preliminary model with flights and cities — the property graph

This might seem to be a fair model, however, there are a few problems with the approach. Relationships, in graphs, are used to model how the entities' nodes are related to each other. As discussed earlier, flights are one of the two core entities in our model. Flights don't *relate* cities to each other, instead, they are a means to get from one city to another. Modeling flights as relationships, can work out in presenting a flight plan, but if we have to allow flight bookings in the future, then we need to change flights to nodes. In general, it's always a good practice to model any entity in the domain as a node. *Figure 2.4* shows us an alternative approach to model flights and cities.

 Modeling entities as relationships must be avoided. Relationships in Neo4j can't have other relationships linked to them. Relationships should depict semantically relevant connections between two entities, not entities themselves.

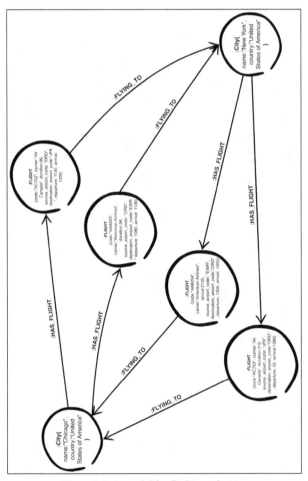

Figure 2.4: A model for flights and cities

The preceding data model has **:Flight** and **:City** as labels for the nodes for flights and cities, respectively. **:HAS_FLIGHT** and **:FLYING_TO** are relationships that link a flight to its origin city and destination city, respectively.

When we represent a part of a graph that contains all possible nodes and relationships, we lay down a specification for how data is connected and structured. Thus, we can describe graphs using specification by example.

This graph seems to be a good starting point for us to begin feeding the data into Neo4j.

Before we move forward, it would be a good idea to install Neo4j so that we can work on the Cypher queries. Neo4j can be downloaded from http://neo4j.com/download/.

Once installed, we will use the **neo4j-shell**, a console tool for Neo4j to create nodes and relationships. Further in this book, we will make use of the Neo4j Browser tool, when we start dealing with traversal and exploring our graph. Before trying out any of the queries, ensure that the Neo4j server is started.

Using Cypher to operate on Neo4j

Operations on Neo4j are generally performed using a query language called Cypher. Cypher is a simple, expressive, SQL-like language that allows us to create, read, update, and delete nodes and relationships in Neo4j. To retrieve data from a Neo4j store, we write Cypher queries, which specify which nodes and which relationships to traverse.

Cypher is a declarative graph query language. Each query is built of clauses and each clause pipes/feeds the next clause with data. Cypher is designed to be a humane query language suitable for developers and operations professionals, and hence, elegantly combines simplicity, expressiveness. and efficiency.

There are ways in which you can, and should influence efficiency from a user perspective, particularly by writing queries that utilize and are sympathetic to the graph structure. However, each query is planned, costed, and executed by the query engine that tries to optimize queries. This allows users to focus on better modeling rather than worrying about the optimization of the queries being written.

To start with, we will need the following clauses:

- CREATE: This clause is used to create nodes and relationships.
- MATCH: This clause matches a certain set of nodes and relationships following the patterns specified.
- RETURN: This decides which part of the created data should be returned. It can be used to return nodes, relationships, or even individual properties.

Before we move forward, we need to ensure that we have a working Neo4j installation.

There are other tools such as Gremlin and the Java API that can be used to query and operate on Neo4j. We feel that Cypher is the most expressive among all of these options. Cypher, however, has limitations to processing which Gremlin addresses better. Gremlin, is not officially supported as of 2.2.0, and Neo4j requires a plugin to execute Cypher queries

Creating cities in Neo4j

We will model cities as nodes, as shown in *Figure 2.4*, with the city's name and country as properties. Cities should have unique names. For this, we can add a constraint before we start creating cities in our graph.

The query is as follows:

```
neo4j-sh (?)$ CREATE CONSTRAINT ON (city: City) ASSERT
  city.name IS UNIQUE;
```

The output of the preceding query is as shown:

```
+--------------------+
| No data returned.  |
+--------------------+
Constraints added: 1
```

This adds a constraint on all nodes that will henceforth be created with the label City to have a unique name property. The city in (city: City) is a placeholder, like a variable, for any node with label City. Note that the addition of a uniqueness constraint is idempotent—it can be repeated multiple times without throwing an error or changing the constraint after it first gets added.

It's a good practice to add a uniqueness constraint, like we did, before we start adding nodes that have a particular label. While a uniqueness constraint can be added anytime, creating one beforehand ensures that no two nodes with the same label will have the same identifier. Currently, there is no way to specify a uniqueness constraint that combines multiple fields. However, we can have multiple uniqueness constraints on the label. To emulate a uniqueness constraint that spans multiple properties, we can create a property that combines the values of two properties and creates a new constraint on this property with joint values. For example, if cities have unique names within the context of a country, we can create a property with the city name and country name appended and create a uniqueness constraint on that.

The primary function of a label is to provide semantic context for nodes. As discussed earlier, a node can have multiple labels, because a node can represent multiple things to the same system. As a corollary, a node can have multiple uniqueness constraints applied to it in context of the different labels applied to it. Labels can be added or removed from a node.

While allowing for uniqueness constraints isn't the primary role of labels, it is important to note that without labels, adding uniqueness constraints isn't possible.

We can add our first city—New York as shown here:

```
neo4j-sh (?)$ CREATE (city:City{name:"New York",
  country:"United States of America"}) RETURN n;
```

The output is as follows:

```
+-------------------------------------------------------------+
| n                                                           |
+-------------------------------------------------------------+
| Node[1]{name:"New York",country:"United States of America"} |
+-------------------------------------------------------------+
1 row
Nodes created: 1
Properties set: 2
Labels added: 1
```

In the query, city is a variable name just like n or x. While it can be anything, we recommend usage of readable and meaningful variable names in the query. We use variable names to ensure that we are referring to the same set of nodes, to use them in multiple parts of the query.

The output of each query on the Neo4j console can be divided into three parts:

- **Variable name**: This is the name of the value that is returned by the query.

- **Variable values**: These are the values that are returned by the query.

- **Modification summary**: This includes how much data is returned, everything that was (or not) modified, and the time taken to run the query.

> The ID of the node created, is a part of the output, but should never be used to identify the node uniquely. Neo4j recycles IDs of any nodes that have been deleted. For example, if we delete the node we just created, the ID (1) of the node will be added to the free pool, and next time the server restarts, it might be reassigned to some other node we might create. Thus, using the generated Neo4j ID to identify a node is risky.

We can also create multiple cities in the same query with the following code:

```
neo4j-sh (?)$ CREATE
  (:City{name:"Mumbai", country:"India"}),
  (:City{name:"Chicago",
  country:"United States of America"}),
  (:City{name:"Las Vegas", country:"United States
  of America"}),(:City{name:"Los Angeles",
  country:"United States of America"}),
  (:City{name:"Toronto", country:"Canada"}),
  (:City{name:"London", country:"United Kingdom"}),
  (:City{name:"Madrid", country:"Spain"}),
  (:City{name:"Paris", country:"France"}),
  (:City{name:"Athens", country:"Greece"}),
  (:City{name:"Rome", country:"Italy"}),
  (:City{name:"Istanbul", country:"Turkey"}),
  (:City{name:"Singapore", country:"Singapore"}),
  (:City{name:"Sydney", country:"Australia"}),
  (:City{name:"Melbourne", country:"Australia"});
```

The output of the previous query is as follows:

```
+--------------------+
| No data returned.  |
+--------------------+
Nodes created: 14
Properties set: 28
Labels added: 14
```

We can retrieve the cities we just created by using the following query:

```
neo4j-sh (?)$ MATCH (city:City{name:"New York"}) RETURN city;
```

The output of this query is as follows:

```
+-----------------------------------------------------------------+
| city                                                            |
+-----------------------------------------------------------------+
| Node[1]{country:"United States of America",name:"New York"}    |
+-----------------------------------------------------------------+
1 row
```

We can also retrieve multiple cities in the same query as shown here:

```
neo4j-sh (?)$ MATCH (c1:City{name:"Athens"}),
    (c2:City{name:"Mumbai"}) RETURN c1, c2;
```

The output is as follows:

```
+-----------------------------------------------------------------+
| c1                                  | c2                        |
+-----------------------------------------------------------------+
| Node[7]{name:"Athens",country:"Greece"}                         |
  Node[9]{name:"Mumbai",country:"India"}                          |
+-----------------------------------------------------------------+
1 row
```

While we can return whole nodes as our result, it's generally advised to return only the data that is needed. It's also possible to alias the data that is returned. The following query returns the names of two cities as shown:

```
neo4j-sh (?)$ MATCH (c1:City{name:"Athens"}),
    (c2:City{name:"Mumbai"}) RETURN c1.name as
    first_city, c2.name as second_city;
```

The output is as follows:

```
+---------------------------+
| first_city | second_city |
+---------------------------+
| "Athens"   | "Mumbai"    |
+---------------------------+
1 row
```

Indices

We have added a property `country` to every node labeled as `City`. We can search for cities belonging to a country as well. Searching without indexes is inefficient, and hence, it's a good practice to add an index for properties which we anticipate the nodes will be searched by. Let's see how this is done using an example as shown:

```
neo4j-sh (?)$ CREATE INDEX ON :City(country);
```

The output is as follows:

```
+--------------------+
| No data returned.  |
+--------------------+
Indexes added: 1
```

Creating an index returns `Indexes added: 1`. However, at this point, an index may not have been added — but will be created. In our database, an index would already have been created. In larger datasets, the indexing will take time.

The index we have just created is called **schema index**.

 Whenever we send Neo4j a Cypher query for execution, Neo4j will try reducing the queried graph to a small subgraph, and then try comparing which nodes have `properties:value` queried. In larger databases, the subgraph itself might have millions of nodes, and checking each node within the subgraph for the presence of the `property:value` pair would be time consuming. To avoid store scans, and to improve discrete lookup performance, we can declare an index on properties for a given label. It is also a good practice to restrict the subgraph using the label of the nodes we want the query to operate on. Since labels are indexed by default, finding nodes using labels is fast for Neo4j.

We can now search for cities in a country without worrying about performance. For example, to search all cities in the United States of America we will use the following query:

```
neo4j-sh (?)$ MATCH (c:City{country:"United States
  of America"}) RETURN c.name as City;
```

The output is as follows:

```
+---------------+
| City          |
+---------------+
| "Las Vegas"   |
| "New York"    |
| "Los Angeles" |
| "Chicago"     |
+---------------+
4 rows
```

Adding flights to Neo4j

Since we have identified flights as entities, we will create them as nodes. To begin with, we should create a uniqueness constraint on the property code for the label :Flight as shown:

```
neo4j-sh (?)$ CREATE CONSTRAINT ON (flight:Flight)
    ASSERT flight.code IS UNIQUE;
```

The output is as follows:

```
+-------------------+
| No data returned. |
+-------------------+
Constraints added: 1
```

We can create a flight with its information as a standalone entity:

```
neo4j-sh (?)$ CREATE (flight:Flight {code:"AA9",
    carrier:"American Airlines", duration:314,
    source_airport_code:"JFK", departure:1300,
    destination_airport_code:"LAX", arrival:114})
    RETURN flight.code as flight_code,
    flight.carrier as carrier, flight.source_airport_code
    as from, flight.destination_airport_code as to;
```

The output is as follows:

```
+---------------------------------------------------+
| flight_code | carrier              | from  | to    |
+---------------------------------------------------+
| "AA9"       | "American Airlines"  | "JFK" | "LAX" |
+---------------------------------------------------+
1 row
Nodes created: 1
Properties set: 5
Labels added: 1
```

This flight can now be connected to the source and destination cities by means of relationships. Relationships in Neo4j must have a direction while being created. In the absence of a specified direction while creation, the query will throw an error. Here's an example:

```
neo4j-sh (?)$ MATCH (source:City {name:"New York"}),
   (destination:City {name:"Los Angeles"}),
   (flight:Flight{code:"AA9"})
   CREATE (source)-[:HAS_FLIGHT]->(flight)-[:FLYING_TO]-(destination);
```

The output of this query is as follows:

```
WARNING: Only directed relationships are supported
   in CREATE (line 1, column 164 (offset: 163))
"MATCH (source:City {name:"New York"}),
   (destination:City {name:"Los Angeles"}),
   (flight:Flight{code:"AA9"})CREATE (source)-[:HAS_FLIGHT]
   ->(flight)-[:FLYING_TO]-(destination)"
```

In the preceding example, we don't have a direction specified on the [:FLYING_TO] relationship.

If we provide a direction to the relationship in the Cypher query, Neo4j will create the relationship in the database.

Input the following query:

```
neo4j-sh (?)$ MATCH (source:City {name:"New York"}),
   (destination:City {name:"Los Angeles"}),
   (flight:Flight{code:"AA9"})CREATE (source)-[:HAS_FLIGHT]
   ->(flight)-[:FLYING_TO]->(destination);
```

The output obtained is as follows:

```
+-------------------+
| No data returned. |
+-------------------+
Relationships created: 2
Properties set: 2
```

The structure of the query is simple. We select the nodes that need to be linked and then create a relationship between them. In the preceding example, source, destination and flight represent variables that are temporarily used to hold the nodes between which the relationships have to be formed. :HAS_FLIGHT and :FLYING_TO are both relationship types. As discussed earlier, relationships can have properties.

> The type of a relationship is tied to the relationship. They are like labels in the semantic sense, but once a relationship is created with a type, it cannot be changed, nor can more types be added.
>
> The direction of the relationship is denoted by the direction in which the arrow (->) points. Both the direction and type are intrinsic to the relationship, and to change any of these, we need to delete the relationship and recreate it with the desired type and direction.

These two steps of creating the flight and then connecting them to the cities can be condensed into one by writing a slightly longer query, as shown here:

```
neo4j-sh (?)$ CREATE (flight:Flight {code:"AA920",
    carrier:"American Airlines", duration:305,
    source_airport_code:"LAX", departure:505,
    destination_airport_code:"JFK", arrival:990})
WITH flight
MATCH (source:City {name:"Los Angeles"}),
    (destination:City {name:"New York"})
CREATE (source)-[:HAS_FLIGHT]->
    (flight)-[:FLYING_TO]->(destination);
```

The output of this query is as follows:

```
+-------------------+
| No data returned. |
+-------------------+
Nodes created: 1
Relationships created: 2
Properties set: 7
Labels added: 1
```

In the preceding query, we used WITH to pipe the result of the first part of the query to the second.

Let's create a few more flights using the queries in `flights.cqy`, which we downloaded at the beginning of this chapter.

Traversing relationships

Traversing relationships in Neo4j is done by specifying the path that we want to be matched. Queries can be open ended, like the one here, in which we haven't highlighted the direction in which we want the relationship to be traversed. Other open-ended queries might refrain from specifying the relationship type to be traversed or the node labels that would identify the subgraph that needs to be traversed.

Input the following query:

```
neo4j-sh (?)$ MATCH (source:City {name:"Los Angeles"})
  ->[:HAS_FLIGHT]-(f:Flight)-[:FLYING_TO]->
  (destination:City {name:"New York"})
  RETURN f.code as flight_code, f.carrier as carrier;
```

The output of this query is as follows:

```
+-----------------------------------+
| flight_code | carrier             |
+-----------------------------------+
| "UA1262"    | "United"            |
| "AA920"     | "American Airlines" |
+-----------------------------------+
2 rows
```

Summary

In this chapter, you learned that graphs can be described by describing a subgraph that contains all possible relationships, nodes, and properties; this is called specification by example. You also learned that entities should be modeled as nodes, and relationships must be used to denote semantic correlation between two entities. Nodes can have multiple labels, while relationships can have only one type. We also discussed the advantages of using labels apart from the semantic context they provide.

3
Formulating an Itinerary

In the previous chapter, you learned to visualize a domain as a graph and how to feed it into Neo4j using **Cypher**. This chapter will revolve around using that data to get the desired information. This can be done using Cypher to query the graph and return the desired data. You will learn the following:

- Querying using Cypher for variable length relationships
- Using functions to extract data from a collection of nodes
- What operations are suited for Cypher

Creating an itinerary from flights and cities

We modelled cities and flights in the previous chapter. In this chapter, our primary focus will be on creating an itinerary from the graph we have. A few considerations while we are fetching the itinerary are as follows:

- Even if there is no direct flight from city A to city B, most people are comfortable with two or less stopovers/changes of flights
- If there is a change of flights or stopover involved, the stopover should be at least for two hours so that the travelers can change flights in spite of any unforeseen delays

Information and paths

In a graph, we discover information by traversing the nodes and relationships from some starting node or nodes. Collectively, the start node, the end node, the relationships, and intermediate nodes together consist of a **path**. We define the path using the node labels and relationship types. Writing queries with node labels and relationship types allows the query to be expressive.

Using Cypher to find a path

In order to find flights, we can use the clauses that we used in the previous chapter. In addition to the MATCH and RETURN clause, we will use the WITH clause and collection functions. A short description of each of these is as follows:

- The MATCH clause is used to match a path having the specified node and relationship types.

- The RETURN clause is used to return the matched path, a few nodes/relationships, or properties from nodes/relationships in the path.

- Collection functions are used to extract data from a collection of nodes that the MATCH clause or other collection functions return.

- The WITH clause is used to pipe the results from one logical part of the query to another logical part. It can be combined with usage of.

We already wrote a query to find flights between two cities.

The query to find a flight path is a simple extension of the query to find one flight.

To visualize paths, we are going to use the Neo4j browser. It is a better tool compared to the neo4j-shell to visualize connected data. For queries where we return a couple of properties, the neo4j-shell is still a tool of choice.

The query to be written is:

```
MATCH path = (london:City{name:'London'})-[:HAS_FLIGHT|FLYING_
TO*0..6]->(melbourne:City{name:'Melbourne'}) RETURN path;
```

The following screenshot shows you the output of the preceding query:

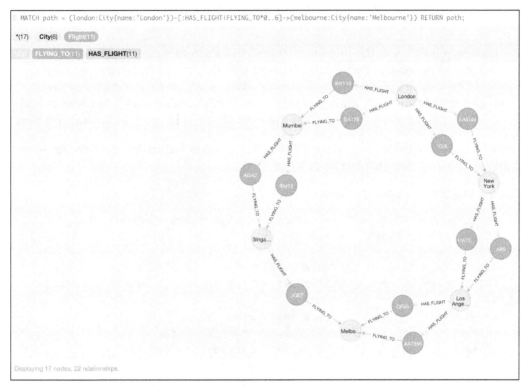

Figure. 3.1: Flights from London to Melbourne

If we compare this with the query to find a flight between New York and London, you will notice that we have eliminated the mention of the flight node, and instead specified a pattern of relationships to match. The pipe symbol (|) separating the relationship types is used to specify multiple relationships that might be matched by the query. The asterisk (∗) and the range after it specify the relationship-node hops the query should be traversing.

In cases where the graph has cycles, usage of * along with the specification of the depth should be carefully thought out. A carefully thought out query with both lower bound and upper bound of the traversal will return useful data, while a query that has been hacked together without much thought might not return any data. In some cases, if the query runs into a cycle and has no upper bound for the query depth, the JVM might crash.

We have specified six as the maximum number of hops to be taken. This number is the result of an assumption made earlier in this chapter; most people would be comfortable with at the most two stopovers. This translates to at most three flight changes. Considering each flight has two relationships connecting it to a source and destination city, we have to traverse at the most six hops in order to get our itinerary.

It is good practice to just return the information needed for further processing rather than returning the whole path from Neo4j.

The input query is as shown here:

```
MATCH path = (london:City{name:'London'})-[:HAS_FLIGHT|FLYING_
TO*0..6]->(melbourne:City{name:'Melbourne'})
WITH
FILTER(f in nodes(path) WHERE  "Flight" IN labels(f)) as flights,
FILTER(city in nodes(path) WHERE "City" IN labels(city)) as cities
RETURN
EXTRACT(city IN cities| city.name) as city,
EXTRACT (flight IN flights| flight.code) as code,
EXTRACT (flight IN flights| flight.carrier) as carrier,
EXTRACT (flight IN flights| flight.departure) as departure,
EXTRACT (flight IN flights| flight.arrival) as arrival,
EXTRACT (flight IN flights| flight.duration) as duration,
EXTRACT (flight IN flights| flight.source_airport_code) as from_
airport,
EXTRACT (flight IN flights| flight.destination_airport_code) as to_
airport
```

The output for the preceding code is as follows:

city	code	carrier	departure	arrival	duration	from_airport	to_airport
[London, New York, Los Angeles, Melbourne]	[AA6144, AA9, AA7356]	[American Airlines, American Airlines, American Airlines]	[1085, 1300, 1370]	[1255, 114, 515]	[535, 314, 945]	[LHR, JFK, LAX]	[JFK, LAX, MEL]
[London, New York, Los Angeles, Melbourne]	[VS9, AA9, AA7356]	[Virgin Atlantic, American Airlines, American Airlines]	[965, 1300, 1370]	[1130, 114, 515]	[535, 314, 945]	[LHR, JFK, LAX]	[JFK, LAX, MEL]
[London, New York, Los Angeles, Melbourne]	[AA6144, UA1507, AA7356]	[American Airlines, United, American Airlines]	[1085, 720, 1370]	[1255, 900, 515]	[535, 300, 945]	[LHR, JFK, LAX]	[JFK, LAX, MEL]
[London, New York, Los Angeles, Melbourne]	[VS9, UA1507, AA7356]	[Virgin Atlantic, United, American Airlines]	[965, 720, 1370]	[1130, 900, 515]	[535, 300, 945]	[LHR, JFK, LAX]	[JFK, LAX, MEL]
[London, New York, Los Angeles, Melbourne]	[AA6144, AA9, QF95]	[American Airlines, American Airlines, Quantas]	[1085, 1300, 1370]	[1255, 114, 515]	[535, 314, 945]	[LHR, JFK, LAX]	[JFK, LAX, MEL]
[London, New York, Los Angeles, Melbourne]	[VS9, AA9, QF95]	[Virgin Atlantic, American Airlines, Quantas]	[965, 1300, 1370]	[1130, 114, 515]	[535, 314, 945]	[LHR, JFK, LAX]	[JFK, LAX, MEL]
[London, New York, Los Angeles, Melbourne]	[AA6144, UA1507, QF95]	[American Airlines, United, Quantas]	[1085, 720, 1370]	[1255, 900, 515]	[535, 300, 945]	[LHR, JFK, LAX]	[JFK, LAX, MEL]
[London, New York, Los Angeles, Melbourne]	[VS9, UA1507, QF95]	[Virgin Atlantic, United, Quantas]	[965, 720, 1370]	[1130, 900, 515]	[535, 300, 945]	[LHR, JFK, LAX]	[JFK, LAX, MEL]
[London, Mumbai, Singapore, Melbourne]	[9W119, AI342, JQ07]	[Jet, Air India, Jetstar]	[1280, 1, 1260]	[660, 465, 405]	[550, 315, 405]	[LHR, BOM, SIN]	[BOM, SIN, MEL]
[London, Mumbai, Singapore, Melbourne]	[BA176, AI342, JQ07]	[British Airways, Air India, Jetstar]	[625, 1, 1260]	[1430, 465, 405]	[535, 315, 405]	[LHR, BOM, SIN]	[BOM, SIN, MEL]
[London, Mumbai, Singapore, Melbourne]	[9W119, 9W12, JQ07]	[Jet, Jet, Jetstar]	[1280, 80, 1260]	[660, 570, 405]	[550, 340, 405]	[LHR, BOM, SIN]	[BOM, SIN, MEL]
[London, Mumbai, Singapore, Melbourne]	[BA176, 9W12, JQ07]	[British Airways, Jet, Jetstar]	[625, 80, 1260]	[1430, 570,	[535, 340,	[LHR, BOM,	[BOM, SIN,

Returned 12 rows in 126 ms.

Figure. 3.2: Information of flights from London to Melbourne

Business logic should lie in code

We returned data from Neo4j without any processing such as ordering flights by their duration or only choosing those connecting flights that are flying out at least two hours after the arrival of the incoming flight. There are multiple reasons for this:

- Returning flights or itineraries sorted by flight duration doesn't solve anything for us since the total journey time will be a sum of all the flight durations and all the layovers.

- Eager aggregation is generally an expensive process and, in case the client consuming data from Neo4j has processing power, it's better to delegate the processing to the client rather than do it in Neo4j.

- In our case specifically, the aggregation for layover times is a complex calculation, more suited to programming languages rather than a query language such as Cypher.

- The minimum layover time of two hours is more of a business logic and needs to be tackled in code and not on the database. In general, it's better to keep queries and business logic separate.

Summary

In this chapter, you learned how to query multiple hop paths and set limits of hops that we have to traverse. You also learned to use functions to extract data from a set of collections. In the next chapter, you will learn how to redesign the existing data.

4
Modeling Bookings and Users

In the previous chapters, you learned how to model flights, reviews, comments, and users. We used a graph to find routes between two cities. However, we limited ourselves to problems that naturally fit into a graph, that is, routing. In this chapter, we will explore how graphs can be used to solve problems that are dominantly solved using RDBMS, for example, bookings.

We will discuss the following topics in this chapter:

- Modeling bookings in an RDBMS
- Modeling bookings in a graph
- Adding bookings to graphs
- Using Cypher to find bookings and journeys

Building a data model for booking flights

We have a graph that allows people to search flights. At this point, a logical extension to the problem statement could be to allow users to book flights online after they decide the route on which they wish to travel. We were only concerned with flights and the cities. However, we need to tweak the model to include users, bookings, dates, and capacity of the flight in order to make bookings. Most teams choose to use an RDBMS for sensitive data such as user information and bookings. Let's understand how we can translate a model from an RDBMS to a graph.

A flight booking generally has many moving parts. While it would be great to model all of the parts of a flight booking, a smaller subset would be more feasible, to demonstrate how to model data that is normally stored in a RDBMS.

A flight booking will contain information about the user who booked it along with the date of booking. It's not uncommon to change multiple flights to get from one city to another. We can call these journey legs or journeys, and model them separately from the booking that has these journeys. It is also possible that the person booking the flight might be booking for some other people. Because of this, it is advisable to model passengers with their basic details separately from the user.

 We have intentionally skipped details such as payment and costs in order to keep the model simple.

A simple model of the bookings ecosystem

A booking generally contains information such as the date of booking, the user who booked it, and a date of commencement of the travel. A journey contains information about the flight code. Other information about the journey such as the departure and arrival time, and the source and destination cities can be evaluated on the basis of the flight which the journey is being undertaken. Both booking and journey will have their own specific IDs to identify them uniquely. Passenger information related to the booking must have the name of the passengers at the very least, but more commonly will have more information such as the age, gender, and e-mail.

A rough model of the **Booking, Journey, Passenger,** and **User** looks like this:

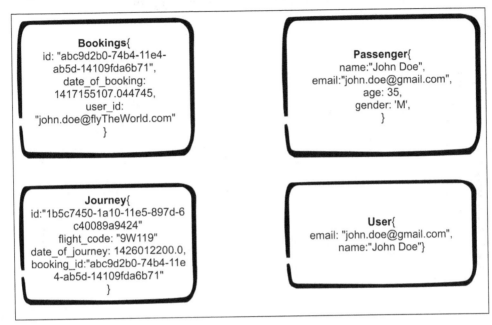

Figure 4.1: Bookings ecosystem

Modeling bookings in an RDBMS

To model data shown in *Figure 4.1* in an RDBMS, we will have to create tables for bookings, journeys, passengers, and users. In the previous model, we have intentionally added `booking_id` to **Journeys** and `user_id` to **Bookings**. In an RDBMS, these will be used as foreign keys.

We also need an additional table `Bookings_Passengers_Relationships` so that we can depict the many relationships between Bookings and Passengers. The multiple relationships between Bookings and Passengers help us to ensure that we capture passenger details for two purposes. The first is that a user can have a master list of travelers they have travelled with and the second use is to ensure that all the journeys taken by a person can be fetched when the passenger logs into their account or creates an account in the future.

We are naming the foreign key references with a prefix fk_ in adherence to the popular convention.

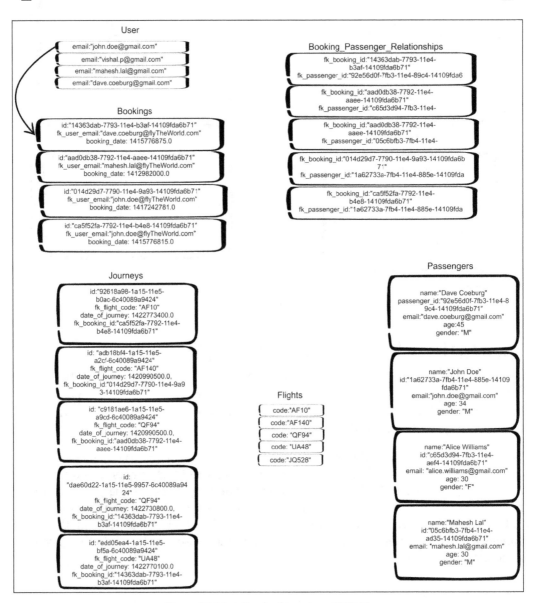

Figure 4.2: Modeling bookings in an RDBMS

In an RDBMS, every record is a representation of an entity (or a relationship in case of relationship tables). In our case, we tried to represent a single booking record as a single block. This applies to all other entities in the system, such as the journeys, passengers, users, and flights. Each of the records has its own ID by which it can be uniquely identified. The properties starting with `fk_` are foreign keys, which should be present in the tables to which the key points.

In our model, passengers may or may not be the users of our application. Hence, we don't add a foreign key constraint to the **Passengers** table. To infer whether the passenger is one of the users or not, we will have to use other means of inferences, for example, the e-mail ID. Given the relationships of the data, which are inferred using the foreign key relationships and other indirect means, we can draw the logical graph of bookings as shown in the following diagram:

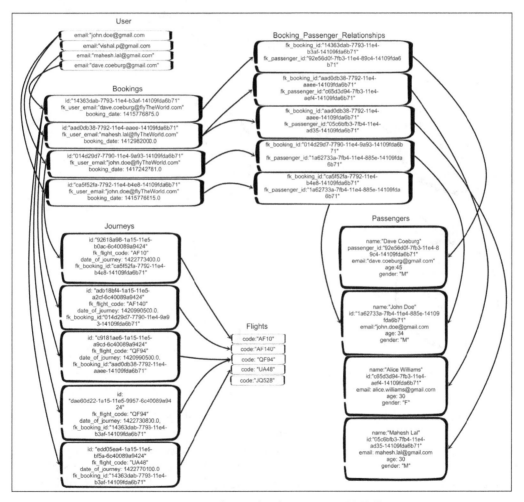

Figure 4.3: Visualizing related entities in an RDBMS

Figure 4.3 shows us the logical graph of how entities are connected in our domain. We can translate this into a **Bookings** subgraph. In *Chapter 2, Modeling Flights and Cities*, we briefly touched upon specification by example. From the related entities of *Figure 4.3*, we can create a specification of the **Bookings** subgraph, which is as follows:

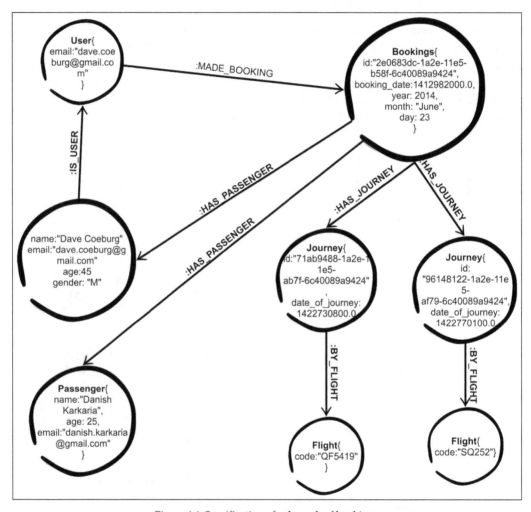

Figure 4.4: Specification of subgraph of bookings

Comparing *Figure 5.3* and *Figure 5.4*, we observe that all the `fk_` properties are removed from the nodes that represent the entities. Since we have explicit relationships that can now be used to traverse the graph, we don't need implicit relationships that rely on foreign keys to be enforced. We put the date of booking on the booking itself rather than on the relationship between **User** and **Bookings**.

The date of booking can be captured either in the booking node or in the `:MADE_BOOKING` relationship. The advantage of capturing it in the booking node is that we can further run queries efficiently on it rather than relying on crude filtering methods to extract information from the subgraph.

An important addition to the **Bookings** object is adding the properties year, month, and day. Since date is not a datatype supported by Neo4j, range queries become difficult. Timestamps solve this problem to some extent, for example, if we want to find all bookings made between June 01, 2015 and July 01, 2015, we can convert them into timestamps and search for all bookings that have timestamps between these two timestamps. This, however, is a very expensive process, and would need a store scan of bookings. To alleviate these problems, we can capture the year, day, and month on the booking.

While adapting to the changing needs of the system, remodeling the data model is encouraged. It is also important that we build a data model with enough data captured for our needs—both current and future. It is a judgment-based decision, without any correct answer. As long as the data might be easily derived from existing data in the node, we recommend not to add it until needed. In this case, converting a timestamp to its corresponding date with its components might require additional programming effort. To avoid that, we can begin capturing the data right away. There might be other cases, for example, we want to introduce a property `Name` on a node with `First name` and `Last name` as properties. The derivation of `Name` from `First name` and `Last name` is straightforward. In this case, we advise not to capture the data till the need arises.

Creating bookings and users in Neo4j

For bookings to exist, we should create users in our data model.

As with earlier chapters, please download the queries from the downloadable code bundle available with this book. Alternatively, the queries can also be downloaded from `https://github.com/maheshlal2910/neo4j_graph_data_modelling`.

Creating users

To create users, we create a constraint on the e-mail of the user, which we will use as an unique identifier as shown in the following query:

```
neo4j-sh (?)$ CREATE CONSTRAINT ON (user:User)
  ASSERT user.email IS UNIQUE;
```

The output of the preceding query is as follows:

```
+-------------------+
| No data returned. |
+-------------------+
Constraints added: 1
```

With the constraint added, let's create a few users in our system:

```
neo4j-sh (?)$ CREATE (:User{name:"Mahesh Lal",
  email:"mahesh.lal@gmail.com"}),
  (:User{name:"John Doe", email:"john.doe@gmail.com"}),
  (:User{name:"Vishal P", email:"vishal.p@gmail.com"}),
  (:User{name:"Dave Coeburg", email:"dave.coeburg@gmail.com"}),
  (:User{name:"Brian Heritage",
    email:"brian.heritage@hotmail.com"}),
  (:User{name:"Amit Kumar", email:"amit.kumar@hotmail.com"}),
  (:User{name:"Pramod Bansal",
    email:"pramod.bansal@hotmail.com"}),
  (:User{name:"Deepali T", email:"deepali.t@gmail.com"}),
  (:User{name:"Hari Seldon", email:"hari.seldon@gmail.com"}),
  (:User{name:"Elijah", email:"elijah.b@gmail.com"});
```

The output of the preceding query is as follows:

```
+-------------------+
| No data returned. |
+-------------------+
Nodes created: 10
Properties set: 20
Labels added: 10
```

[Please add more users from users.cqy.]

Creating bookings in Neo4j

As discussed earlier, a booking has multiple journey legs, and a booking is only complete when all its journey legs are booked.

Bookings in our application aren't a single standalone entity. They involve multiple journeys and passengers. To create a booking, we need to ensure that journeys are created and information about passengers is captured. This results in a multistep process.

To ensure that booking IDs remain unique and no two nodes have the same ID, we should add a constraint on the id property of booking:

```
neo4j-sh (?)$ CREATE CONSTRAINT ON (b:Booking)
    ASSERT b.id IS UNIQUE;
```

The output will be as follows:

```
+-------------------+
| No data returned. |
+-------------------+
Constraints added: 1
```

We will create similar constraints for Journey as shown here:

```
neo4j-sh (?)$ CREATE CONSTRAINT ON (journey:Journey)
    ASSERT journey._id IS UNIQUE;
```

The output is as follows:

```
+-------------------+
| No data returned. |
+-------------------+
Constraints added: 1
```

Add a constraint for the e-mail of passengers to be unique, as shown here:

```
neo4j-sh (?)$ CREATE CONSTRAINT ON (p:Passenger)
    ASSERT p.email IS UNIQUE;
```

The output is as shown:

```
+-------------------+
| No data returned. |
+-------------------+
Constraints added: 1
```

With constraint creation, we can now focus on how bookings can be created. We will be running this query in the Neo4j browser, as shown:

```
//Get all flights and users
MATCH (user:User{email:"john.doe@gmail.com"})
MATCH (f1:Flight{code:"VS9"}), (f2:Flight{code:"AA9"})
//Create a booking for a date
MERGE (user)-[m:MADE_BOOKING]->(booking:Booking
    {_id:"0f64711c-7e22-11e4-a1af-14109fda6b71", booking_
date:1417790677.274862, year: 2014, month: 12, day: 5})
//Create or get passengers
MERGE (p1:Passenger{email:"vishal.p@gmail.com"}) ON CREATE SET p1.name
= "Vishal Punyani", p1.age= 30
MERGE (p2:Passenger{email:"john.doe@gmail.com"}) ON CREATE SET p2.name
= "John Doe",  p2.age= 25
//Create journeys to be taken by flights
MERGE (j1:Journey{_id: "712785b8-1aff-11e5-abd4-6c40089a9424", date_
of_journey:1422210600.0, year:2015, month: 1, day: 26})-[:BY_FLIGHT]->
(f1)
MERGE (j2:Journey{_id:"843de08c-1aff-11e5-8643-6c40089a9424", date_
of_journey:1422210600.0, year:2015, month: 1, day: 26})-[:BY_FLIGHT]->
(f2)
WITH user, booking, j1, j2, f1, f2, p1, p2
//Merge journeys and booking, Create and Merge passengers with
bookings, and return data
MERGE (booking)-[:HAS_PASSENGER]->(p1)
MERGE (booking)-[:HAS_PASSENGER]->(p2)
MERGE (booking)-[:HAS_JOURNEY]->(j1)
MERGE (booking)-[:HAS_JOURNEY]->(j2)
RETURN user, p1, p2, j1, j2, f1, f2, booking
```

The output is as shown in the following screenshot:

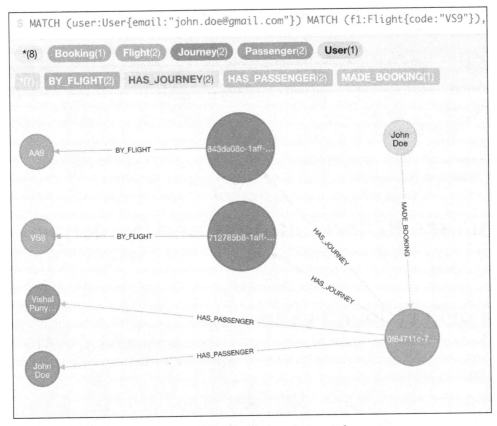

Figure 4.5: Booking that was just created

We have added comments to the query to explain the different parts of the query. The query can be divided into the following parts:

- Finding flights and user
- Creating bookings
- Creating journeys
- Creating passengers and link to booking
- Linking journey to booking

We have the same start date for both journeys, but in general, the start dates of journeys in the same booking will differ if:

- The traveler is flying across time zones. For example, if a traveler is flying from New York to Istanbul, the journeys from New York to London and from London to Istanbul will be on different dates.

- The traveler is booking multiple journeys in which they will be spending some time at a destination.

Let's use `bookings.cqy` to add a few more bookings to the graph. We will use them to run further queries.

Queries to find journeys and bookings

With the data on bookings added in, we can now explore some interesting queries that can help us.

Finding all journeys of a user

All journeys that a user has undertaken will be all journeys that they have been a passenger on. We can use the user's e-mail to search for journeys on which the user has been a passenger.

To find all the journeys that the user has been a passenger on, we should find the journeys via the bookings, and then using the bookings, we can find the journeys, flights, and cities as shown:

```
neo4j-sh (?)$ MATCH (b:Booking)-[:HAS_PASSENGER]-
>(p:Passenger{email:"vishal.p@gmail.com"})
WITH b
MATCH (b)-[:HAS_JOURNEY]->(j:Journey)-[:BY_FLIGHT]->(f:Flight)
WITH b._id as booking_id, j.date_of_journey as date_of_journey,
COLLECT(f) as flights ORDER BY date_of_journey DESC
MATCH (source:City)-[:HAS_FLIGHT]->(f)-[:FLYING_TO]-
>(destination:City)
WHERE f in flights
RETURN booking_id, date_of_journey, source.name as from, f.code as by_
flight, destination.name as to;
```

The output of this query is as follows:

booking_id	date_of_journey	from	by_flight	to
f87a515e-7e2d-11e4-b170-14109fda6b71	1431196200	Los Angeles	AA920	New York
ccc84f47-7e28-11e4-90c4-14109fda6b71	1426617000	New York	UA1507	Los Angeles
b5489547-7e24-11e4-b327-14109fda6b71	1426357800	Mumbai	UA49	New York
fef04c30-7e2d-11e4-8842-14109fda6b71	1422642600	New York	VS8	London
0f64711c-7e22-11e4-a1af-14109fda6b71	1422210600	London	VS9	New York
0f64711c-7e22-11e4-a1af-14109fda6b71	1422210600	New York	AA9	Los Angeles

While this query is useful to get all the journeys of the user, it can also be used to map all the locations the user has travelled to.

Queries to find the booking history of a user

The query for finding all bookings by a user is straightforward, as shown here:

```
neo4j-sh (?)$ MATCH (user:User{email:"mahesh.lal@gmail.com"})-[:MADE_
BOOKING]->(b:Booking) RETURN b._id as booking_id;
```

The output of the preceding query is as follows:

```
+------------------------------------------+
| booking_id                               |
+------------------------------------------+
| "251679be-1b3f-11e5-820e-6c40089a9424"   |
| "ff3dd694-7e7f-11e4-bb93-14109fda6b71"   |
| "7c63cc35-7e7f-11e4-8ffe-14109fda6b71"   |
| "f5f15252-1b62-11e5-8252-6c40089a9424"   |
| "d45de0c2-1b62-11e5-98a2-6c40089a9424"   |
| "fef04c30-7e2d-11e4-8842-14109fda6b71"   |
| "f87a515e-7e2d-11e4-b170-14109fda6b71"   |
| "75b3e78c-7e2b-11e4-a162-14109fda6b71"   |
+------------------------------------------+
8 rows
```

Upcoming journeys of a user

Upcoming journeys of a user is straightforward. We can construct it by simply comparing today's date to the journey date as shown:

```
neo4j-sh (?)$ MATCH (user:User{email:"mahesh.lal@gmail.com"})-[:MADE_
BOOKING]->(:Booking)-[:HAS_JOURNEY]-(j:Journey)
WHERE j.date_of_journey >=1418055307
WITH COLLECT(j) as journeys
MATCH (j:Journey)-[:BY_FLIGHT]->(f:Flight)
WHERE j in journeys
WITH j.date_of_journey as date_of_journey, COLLECT(f) as flights
MATCH (source:City)-[:HAS_FLIGHT]->(f)-[:FLYING_TO]-
>(destination:City)
WHERE f in flights
RETURN date_of_journey, source.name as from, f.code as by_flight,
destination.name as to;
```

The output of the preceding query is as follows:

```
+-----------------------------------------------------------------+
| date_of_journey | from          | by_flight | to            |
+-----------------------------------------------------------------+
| 1.4226426E9     | "New York"    | "VS8"     | "London"      |
| 1.4212602E9     | "Los Angeles" | "UA1262"  | "New York"    |
| 1.4212602E9     | "Melbourne"   | "QF94"    | "Los Angeles" |
| 1.4304186E9     | "New York"    | "UA1507"  | "Los Angeles" |
| 1.4311962E9     | "Los Angeles" | "AA920"   | "New York"    |
+-----------------------------------------------------------------+
5 rows
```

Summary

In this chapter, you learned how you can model a domain that has traditionally been implemented using RDBMS. We saw how tables can be changed to nodes and relationships, and we explored what happened to relationship tables. You also learned about transactions in Cypher and wrote Cypher to manipulate the database. In the next chapter, you will learn about refactoring the data models.

5
Refactoring the Data Model

We explored how to model cities and flights in a graph database, and are now able to run queries that return flights and routes for a journey. We also added the capability to book flights to our data model. In this chapter, we will explore how to change the data model to fit new requirements. As we go along, we will explore the following concepts:

- Modifying data model to accommodate business requirements
- Migrating the data from the old model to the new one

Capturing information about hotels at airports

While travelling, if a layover is more than six hours, travelers generally like to rest. Since the travelers might not be possessing a visa for the country that they are transiting through, most dormitories or hotels are located within the airport. As a logical next step, we can capture information about hotels at airports, so that travelers can use the information to plan their journey better. Considering there are multiple airports in a city, it is imperative to show only those hotels that are located at the airport through which the traveler is transiting.

Modeling airports and hotels

To be able to show only those hotels that are located at the airport through which the traveler is transiting, we need to model airports. Currently, airports are a part of the flight information, and this needs to change. We will extract airport information (that is, `airport_code`) into a separate node labeled **:Airport**, as shown in *Figure 5.1*. The property code will act as a unique identifier for an airport.

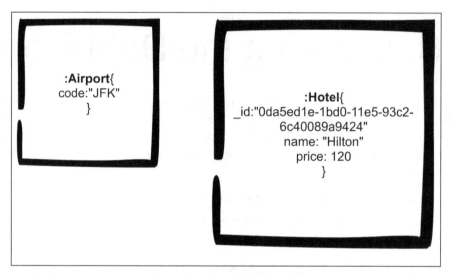

Figure 5.1: Airports and hotels

Hotels will be modeled with their name and the price. Since prices should be comparable, storing them as a number would be beneficial. Considering hotel chains have similar or same names for each class of hotel that that they own, it would be good to have an ID on the hotels.

The currency in which the price is expressed should be a application concern and should not be spread across data and application. Ideally, a standard currency (for example, USD or EUR) would be used to express the price, and the conversion to local currency of the buyer/visitor should be applied in real time depending on the daily market rates.

The following figure shows a subgraph, which specifies the structure of hotels, airports, and cities:

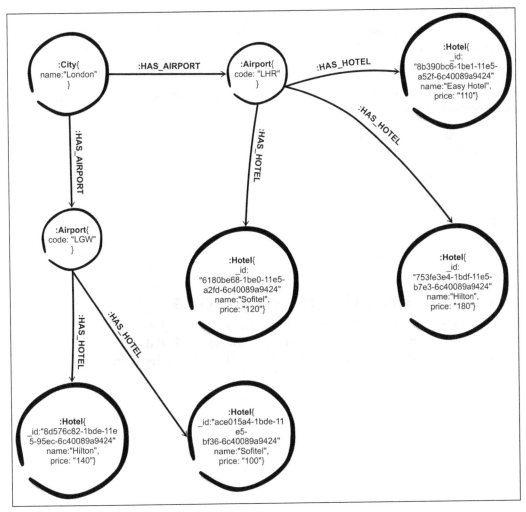

Figure 5.2: Airports and hotels subgraph

Extracting airport information from flights

There are multiple steps involved in making the successful transition from airports being properties of flights to airports being an entity connected to the city they are located in.

To start with, let's create a constraint so that an airport can be uniquely identified by its code. The query is as follows:

```
neo4j-sh (?)$ CREATE CONSTRAINT ON (airport:Airport)
    ASSERT airport.code IS UNIQUE;
```

The output of the preceding query is as follows:

```
+-------------------+
| No data returned. |
+-------------------+
Constraints added: 1
```

Breaking airports out as a node

The next step is to break out the source_airport_code and destination_airport_code properties into nodes. After this change, the **:HAS_FLIGHT** and **:FLYING_TO** relationships will connect **:Flight** and **:Airport** rather than **:Flight** and **:City**, as shown:

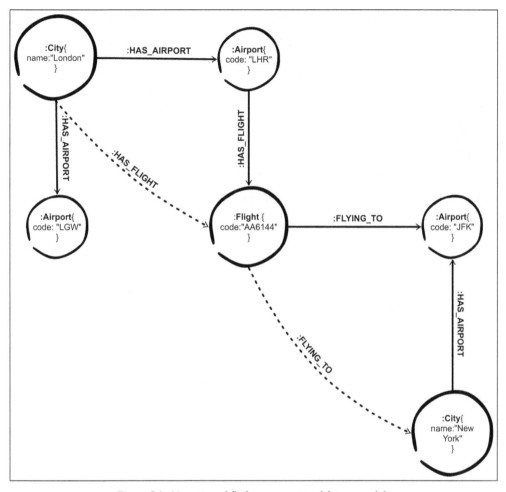

Figure 5.3: Airports and flights—current and future models

In *Figure 5.3*, the relationships depicted with the dotted line exist currently. Relationships shown with a solid line don't exist. Since we haven't started refactoring our graph, airports don't exist. We will have to create airports and then connect the flights to the airports.

We can use the following query to create airports from existing flights:

```
MATCH (source:City)-[:HAS_FLIGHT]->(f:Flight)-[:FLYING_TO]-
>(destination:City)
WITH source, f, destination
MERGE (source_airport:Airport{code: f.source_airport_code})
MERGE (destination_airport:Airport{code: f.destination_airport_code})
WITH source, destination, source_airport, destination_airport
MERGE (source)-[:HAS_AIRPORT]->(source_airport)
MERGE (destination)-[:HAS_AIRPORT]->(destination_airport)
RETURN source, destination, source_airport, destination_airport
```

The output of the preceding query is as shown in the following figure:

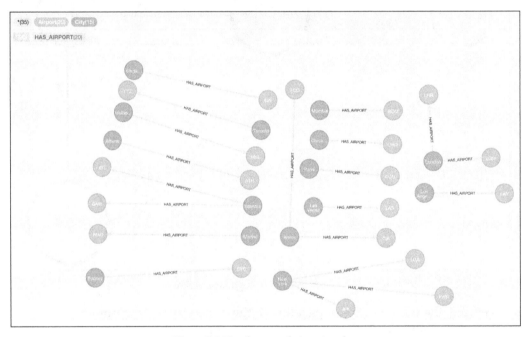

Figure 5.4: Newly created airport nodes

Connecting flights to airports

With the airport nodes separated, we can now connect flights to the airports, using the following code:

```
MATCH (f:Flight)
WITH f
MATCH (source_airport:Airport{code:f.source_airport_code}),
      (destination_airport:Airport{code:f.destination_airport_code})
```

```
WITH  source_airport, destination_airport, f
MERGE (source_airport)-[:HAS_FLIGHT]->(f)-[:FLYING_TO]->(destination_
airport)
RETURN source_airport, f, destination_airport
```

The output of the preceding code is as shown here:

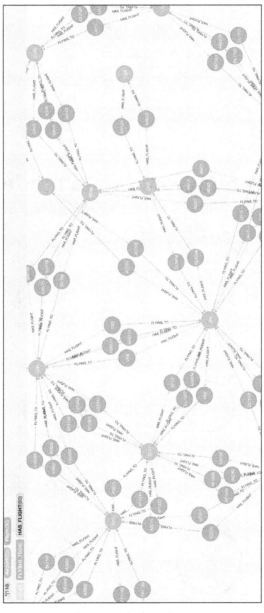

Figure 5.5: Fights connected to airports

Delinking flights and cities

We have now connected flights to airports, and can delink flights and cities. The following query cleans up the relationships between flights and cities, and sets the source and destination codes to null:

```
neo4j-sh (?)$ MATCH (f:Flight)-[r]-(:City)
DELETE r
SET f.source_airport_code = null, f.destination_airport_code = null;
```

The output of the preceding query is as follows:

```
+-----------------------------------------------+
| No data returned                              |
+-----------------------------------------------+
Set 360 properties
Deleted 180 relationships
```

Querying the refactored data model

Our data model has evolved as shown in the following diagram:

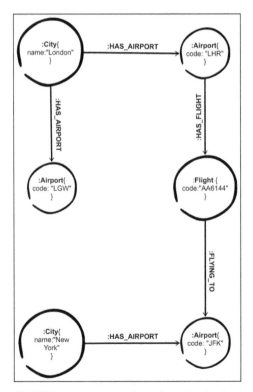

Figure 5.6: Flights and airports after refactoring the data model

With the changes in our data model, we need to change our queries to reflect the addition of airports, as shown here:

```
MATCH path = (london:City{name:'London'})-[:HAS_AIRPORT]->(:Airport)-
[:HAS_FLIGHT|FLYING_TO*0..6]->(:Airport)
<-[:HAS_AIRPORT]-(melbourne:City{name:'Melbourne'})
WITH
FILTER(f in nodes(path) WHERE  "Flight" IN labels(f)) as flights,
FILTER(city in nodes(path) WHERE "City" IN labels(city)) as cities,
FILTER(airport in nodes(path) WHERE "Airport" IN labels(airport)) as
airports
RETURN
EXTRACT(city IN cities| city.name) as city,
EXTRACT (flight IN flights| flight.code) as code,
EXTRACT (flight IN flights| flight.carrier) as carrier,
EXTRACT (flight IN flights| flight.departure) as departure,
EXTRACT (flight IN flights| flight.arrival) as arrival,
EXTRACT (flight IN flights| flight.duration) as duration,
EXTRACT (airport IN airports| airport.code) as airport
```

The output of the preceding code is as follows:

city	code	carrier	departure	arrival	duration	airport
[London, Melbourne]	[AA6144, AA9, AA7356]	[American Airlines, American Airlines, American Airlines]	[1085, 1300, 1370]	[1255, 114, 515]	[535, 314, 945]	[LHR, JFK, LAX, MEL]
[London, Melbourne]	[VS9, AA9, AA7356]	[Virgin Atlantic, American Airlines, American Airlines]	[965, 1300, 1370]	[1130, 114, 515]	[535, 314, 945]	[LHR, JFK, LAX, MEL]
[London, Melbourne]	[AA6144, UA1507, AA7356]	[American Airlines, United, American Airlines]	[1085, 720, 1370]	[1255, 900, 515]	[535, 300, 945]	[LHR, JFK, LAX, MEL]
[London, Melbourne]	[VS9, UA1507, AA7356]	[Virgin Atlantic, United, American Airlines]	[965, 720, 1370]	[1130, 900, 515]	[535, 300, 945]	[LHR, JFK, LAX, MEL]
[London, Melbourne]	[AA6144, AA9, QF95]	[American Airlines, American Airlines, Quantas]	[1085, 1300, 1370]	[1255, 114, 515]	[535, 314, 945]	[LHR, JFK, LAX, MEL]
[London, Melbourne]	[VS9, AA9, QF95]	[Virgin Atlantic, American Airlines, Quantas]	[965, 1300, 1370]	[1130, 114, 515]	[535, 314, 945]	[LHR, JFK, LAX, MEL]
[London, Melbourne]	[AA6144, UA1507, QF95]	[American Airlines, United, Quantas]	[1085, 720, 1370]	[1255, 900, 515]	[535, 300, 945]	[LHR, JFK, LAX, MEL]
[London, Melbourne]	[VS9, UA1507, QF95]	[Virgin Atlantic, United, Quantas]	[965, 720, 1370]	[1130, 900, 515]	[535, 300, 945]	[LHR, JFK, LAX, MEL]
[London, Melbourne]	[BA176, 9W12, JQ07]	[British Airways, Jet, Jetstar]	[625, 80, 1260]	[1430, 570, 405]	[535, 340, 405]	[LHR, BOM, SIN, MEL]
[London, Melbourne]	[9W119, 9W12, JQ07]	[Jet, Jet, Jetstar]	[1280, 80, 1260]	[660, 570, 405]	[550, 340, 405]	[LHR, BOM, SIN, MEL]
[London, Melbourne]	[BA176, AI342, JQ07]	[British Airways, Air India, Jetstar]	[625, 1, 1260]	[1430, 465, 405]	[535, 315, 405]	[LHR, BOM, SIN, MEL]
[London, Melbourne]	[9W119, AI342, JQ07]	[Jet, Air India, Jetstar]	[1280, 1, 1260]	[660, 465, 405]	[550, 315, 405]	[LHR, BOM, SIN, MEL]

Figure 5.7: Flight itinerary

Given our new model, the output format differs slightly. However, the data returned is the same as our last itinerary query in *Chapter 3, Formulating an Itinerary*.

Reasons for not migrating using a single query

Evolution is a constant in the software industry. Most of the times migrations are done, the database and code changes are simultaneous and all of this is deployed in a big bang release. An example of a big bang release in our case would be to make the constraint, make data changes, and delete the relationships in one go. This change will need the code to be deployed along with the changes to the database so that the applications keep running. There are multiple downsides to this approach:

- If something goes wrong at the database end, there might be an outage. A rollback of code will be required along with restoring the database to an earlier state.

- This is more time consuming since it will require a lot more testing and preparation than smaller increments, which can be leak proofed.

If we separate the migration into two steps—constraint and path creation, and relationship removal—we gain the following advantages:

- Since constraint and path creation is done in the first step, we need not deploy the code that has been changed to use the new path at the same time. We can wait and test it further, buying us enough time. Once we are confident about code changes we have made and have released the code to production, we can run the script to remove the relationships that previously represented flights.

- Given that there are no deletions in the first script, anything going wrong won't affect the stability of the application. The cause can be investigated without any downtime.

- Since the deletions in the second script won't affect the subgraph that will be in use by the application, any unfortunate errors won't result in application downtime.

Adding hotels to airports

Now that we have airports as nodes, we can add hotels to our data model. As discussed earlier, hotels have an ID, name, and average price.

Let's start by adding a constraint on the ID of the hotel, which is the _id property, as shown:

```
neo4j-sh (?)$ CREATE CONSTRAINT ON (hotel:Hotel) ASSERT hotel._id IS
UNIQUE;
```

The output of the preceding query is as shown:

```
+-------------------+
| No data returned. |
+-------------------+
Constraints added: 1
```

We can add a hotel and connect it to the JFK airport using the following query:

```
neo4j-sh (?)$ CREATE (hotel:Hotel {_id:"6ad8ce6e-1c0e-11e5-8db1-
6c40089a9424", name:"Hilton", price: 180})
WITH hotel
MATCH (airport:Airport{code:"JFK"})
WITH airport, hotel
MERGE (airport)-[:HAS_HOTEL]->(hotel)
RETURN airport, hotel;
```

The output of the preceding query is as follows:

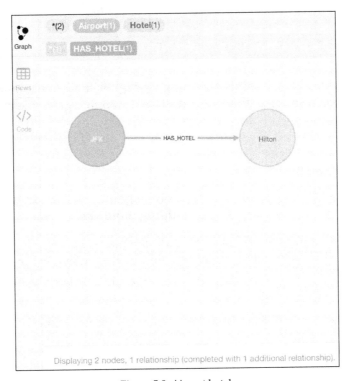

Figure 5.8: Airport hotels

 We can add more hotels from the hotels.cqy file that can be downloaded along with the code for this chapter.

Fetching hotels

Hotels can be found on the basis of which airport are they connected to, as shown in the following query:

```
neo4j-sh (?)$ MATCH (airport:Airport)-[:HAS_HOTEL]->(hotel:Hotel)
WHERE airport.code IN ["JFK", "LAX"]
RETURN airport.code, hotel.name, hotel.price;
```

The output of the preceding query is as follows:

```
+----------------------------------------------------------+
| airport.code | hotel.name            | hotel.price |
+----------------------------------------------------------+
| "JFK"        | "Hampton Inn"         | 70          |
| "JFK"        | "Fairfield Inn"       | 80          |
| "LAX"        | "LAX South Travelodge"| 93          |
| "LAX"        | "Sheraton"            | 170         |
| "LAX"        | "Concourse"           | 100         |
+----------------------------------------------------------+
5 rows
```

Although we can find hotels while searching for flights, it is not necessary. Once the flights have been selected, this is an additional step that gives the travelers some information.

Summary

In this chapter, we explored how we can evolve a graph database in two ways: changing design wherever necessary and adding more varied data.

Adding more varied data should always be for business reasons. Re-design of data might be done for optimizations or could be driven by business reasons. Either of the evolutions are simple to carry out in graph databases like Neo4j, and if planned properly, there is no outage required.

In the next chapter, we will learn about modeling communication chains.

6
Modeling Communication Chains

In the previous chapters, we explored designing a graph that allows a traveler to choose a route of travel, book flights, and also view information about the hotels they might stay at in case they have a long layover. In this chapter, we will explore how can we model reviews for the airport hotels that we introduced in *Chapter 5, Refactoring the Data Model*.

In this chapter, we will explore the following modeling reviews:

- Modeling comments on reviews as chains
- Considerations for modeling temporal data as chains

Capturing traveler reviews for hotels

Currently, among the multiple hotels at any airport, the only parameters that can help a traveler decide on a hotel are the price and the parent chain of the hotel. To compliment these parameters, we can add reviews to help travelers choose a hotel. This gives them multiple parameters to compare hotels and can thus help them choose one based on the parameters important to them. We can choose the following parameters to rate the hotels:

- Food
- Comfort
- Service
- Value for money

To add more context to the rating, we can add a review comment to the review.

There may also be scenarios where other travelers might want to ask the reviewer more questions. For these, we can add comments as separate entities on the review.

A model for reviews and comments

The following figure gives an example of the information that reviews and comments will contain:

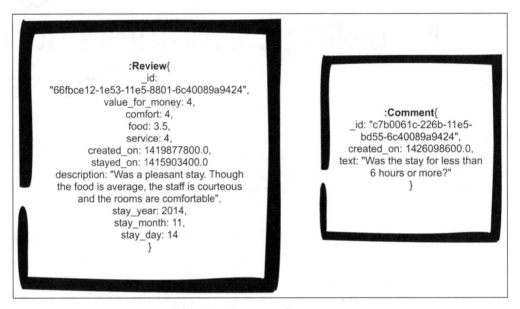

Figure 6.1: Reviews and comments

Every review has to be uniquely identified for which we use the _id property. Value for money, comfort, food, and service are all the parameters that have been discussed earlier. The rating has been given on a scale of 1 to 5, assuming 1 to be lowest and 5 to be the highest. In addition to these, we have created_on, which is the timestamp of the creation of the review. Similarly, stayed_on is a timestamp of the day that the reviewer stayed at the hotel. We also capture additional information such as stay_ year, stay_month, and stay_day. This will help us with range queries on the time of the year that the review was written.

Comments have _id, which uniquely identifies a comment. The created_on property is the timestamp of when the comment was created. The text is the actual communication that the traveler wants to send across to the reviewer.

In the larger ecosystem of cities, airports, hotels, and users, the reviews and comments can be modeled as follows:

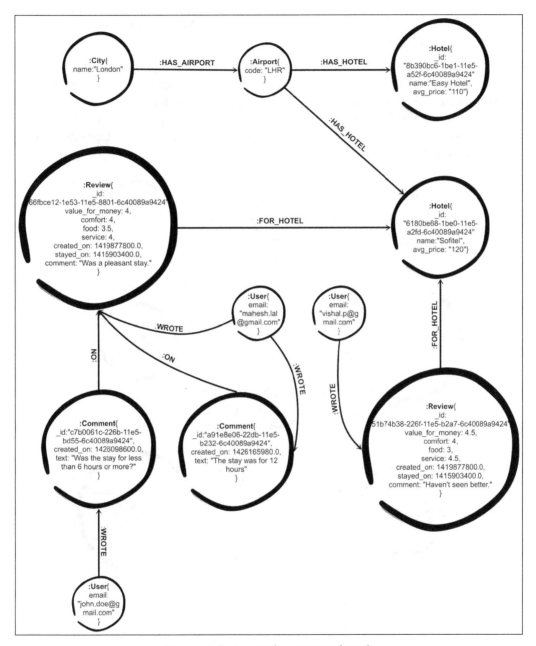

Figure 6.2: Reviews and comments subgraph

Reviews are modeled as nodes and have a **:FOR_HOTEL** relationship with the hotel being reviewed. People comment on a review or on other comments. This can be represented by using an **:ON** relationship between comments and the comment/ review that is being commented on. Users have a **:WROTE** relationship with both reviews and comments.

In our example, comments are used as communication channels between the reviewers and potential travelers. A comment may be a question seeking additional clarification or may be a response. The model doesn't consider the fact that comments might have a temporal relationship between them, for example, a comment might be a reply to another comment. The following figure is a revised design that addresses the relationship between comments:

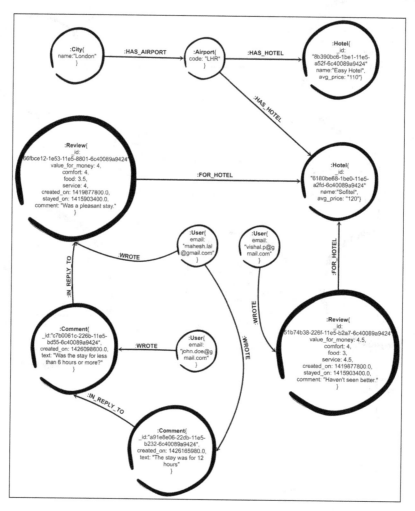

Figure 6.3: Reviews and comments subgraph in which comments are chained

The preceding subgraph suggests that comments should be chained with a **:IN_REPLY_TO** relationship. Modeling comments as chains, allows to explicitly maintain an ordering between them. This way, multiple comments and responses to those comments can be maintained as separate chains. The first comment in a chain will always be **:IN_REPLY_TO** a review. If comments aren't chained, then there is no way to maintain separate questions and responses to them, and it is difficult to find relevant information.

> While reviews also have chronological ordering, they are better modeled as individual reviews related to hotels rather than chaining all reviews of a hotel in some particular order. Reviews are subject to a variety of sorting options, for example, reviews might be sorted by the latest written reviews or by the time of stay. There might be another possible ordering of how the reviews are displayed. Chaining them in reverse chronological order of the time created or the date of stay satisfies one use case, but makes the query for other use cases complicated.

Adding reviews to Neo4j

To add reviews to Neo4j, we should first create an uniqueness constraint on reviews, as shown:

```
neo4j-sh (?)$ CREATE CONSTRAINT ON (review:Review)
  ASSERT review._id IS UNIQUE;
```

The output of the preceding query is as follows:

```
+-------------------+
| No data returned. |
+-------------------+
Constraints added: 1
```

To add a review, we can use the following query:

```
neo4j-sh (?)$ CREATE (review:Review{ _id:
  "d11f1d66-2331-11e5-ab8f-6c40089a9424",
  value_for_money: 2, comfort: 3, food: 4,
  service: 3, stayed_on: 1388670309.210871,
  created_on: 1391157765.857148, stay_year:
  2014, stay_month: 1, stay_day: 2,
  description:"Was a comfortable stay.
  Could improve a lot though"})
WITH review
```

```
MATCH (hotel:Hotel{_id: "19397f48-1c6f-11e5
  -8014-6c40089a9424"}), (user:User {email:
  "mahesh.lal@gmail.com"})
WITH review, user, hotel MERGE (user)-
  [:WROTE]->(review)-[:FOR_HOTEL]->(hotel);
```

The output of the preceding query is as follows:

```
+--------------------+
| No data returned.  |
+--------------------+
Nodes created: 1
Relationships created: 2
Properties set: 11
Labels added: 1
```

 Please add more reviews from the reviews.cqy file that can be found with the code for this chapter. The code can be downloaded from the publisher's website or from https://github.com/maheshlal2910/neo4j_graph_data_modelling. The reviews.cqy file was generated using a script with randomized values, and hence doesn't have a description in each review.

Listing reviews for a hotel

The following query can be used to fetch all reviews for a hotel arranged in reverse chronological order of the reviewer's stay:

```
MATCH (hotel:Hotel{_id:'19397f48-1c6f-11e5-8014
  -6c40089a9424'})<-[:FOR_HOTEL]-(review:Review)
  <-[:WROTE]-(user:User)
WITH review, user, review.stayed_on as
  stayed ORDER BY stayed DESC
RETURN review.value_for_money as value_for_money,
  review.comfort as comfort, review.food as food,
  review.service as service, review.stay_year as year,
  review.stay_month as month, review.stay_day as day,
  user.name as name;
```

The output of the preceding query is as follows:

value_for_money	comfort	food	service	year	month	day	name
1	2	2	2	2015	6	18	Brian Heritage
4	1	3	1	2014	12	20	Amit Kumar
3	1	3	3	2014	9	3	John Doe
3	4	2	4	2014	1	3	Dave Coeburg
2	3	4	3	2014	1	2	Mahesh Lal
2	4	1	4	2013	10	12	Vishal P

Figure 6.4: Reviews for a hotel in reverse chronological order of stay date

Using reviews to find the average rating of a hotel

Now that we have reviews for each hotel, we can get the average rating for each hotel. The following query lists all the hotels in the airports of New York in reverse order of their overall rating:

```
MATCH (city:City{name:"New York"})-[:HAS_AIRPORT]-
    >(airport:Airport)-[:HAS_HOTEL]->(hotel:Hotel)
    <-[:FOR_HOTEL]-(review:Review)
WITH DISTINCT hotel.name AS hotel_name,
COLLECT(review.comfort) AS comfort_ratings,
COLLECT(review.food) AS food_ratings,
COLLECT(review.service) AS service_ratings,
COLLECT(review.value_for_money) as vfm_ratings,
airport.code AS airport,
COUNT(review) as total_reviews

WITH
hotel_name,
tofloat(REDUCE(total = 0, rating in comfort_ratings |
    total + rating))/ total_reviews as comfort_rating,
tofloat(REDUCE(total = 0, rating in food_ratings |
    total + rating))/ total_reviews as food_rating,
tofloat(REDUCE(total = 0, rating in service_ratings |
    total + rating))/ total_reviews as service_rating,
tofloat(REDUCE(total = 0, rating in vfm_ratings |
    total + rating))/ total_reviews as vfm_rating,
airport,
total_reviews
```

```
RETURN airport,
hotel_name,
comfort_rating,
service_rating,
food_rating,
vfm_rating,
(comfort_rating + service_rating + food_rating +
  vfm_rating)/4 as overall_rating
ORDER BY overall_rating DESC
```

The output of the preceding query is as follows:

airport	hotel_name	comfort_rating	service_rating	food_rating	vfm_rating	overall_rating
LGA	LaGuardia Plaza	3	2.5	3.25	2.25	2.75
JFK	Fairfield Inn	2.6	2.8	2	3.4	2.7
JFK	Hampton Inn	2.3333333333333335	2	2.5555555555555554	2.5555555555555554	2.361111111111111
EWR	Wyndham	2.25	2.75	2	1.75	2.1875

Figure 6.5: Hotels ranked by their overall ratings

The preceding query does all of the following:

- Gets all reviews grouped by hotels
- Adds up the individual review parameters for each hotel
- Gets the average individual review parameters by dividing the sum by the total number of reviews
- Calculates the overall rating as the average of all the review parameters

Adding comments to Neo4j

As discussed earlier, comments can be used by users to ask more questions or clarify something to other users. Since chronology is important, we will create a chain for the comments. The assumption here is that for a new question or clarification, a new comment chain will be started with the first comment in the chain being in response to the review being commented on.

Before we add comments, we should set up a constraint on comments to ensure that we don't create comments with the same ID, as shown in the following query:

```
neo4j-sh (?)$ CREATE CONSTRAINT ON (comment:Comment)
  ASSERT comment._id IS UNIQUE;
```

The output of the preceding query is as follows:

```
+-------------------+
| No data returned. |
+-------------------+
Constraints added: 1
```

To add a comment to the review, we can use the following query:

```
CREATE (comment:Comment{_id:"df23c188-2349-11e5-8966-
    6c40089a9424", text:"What was wrong with the service?",
    created_on: 1391550607.342643}))
WITH comment
MATCH (review:Review{_id:"d120a06e-2331-11e5-
    bf11-6c40089a9424"}), (user:User{email:
    "mahesh.lal@gmail.com"})
WITH review, user, comment
MERGE (review)<-[:IN_REPLY_TO]-(comment)
    <-[:WROTE]-(user)
RETURN review, comment, user
```

The output of the preceding query is as follows:

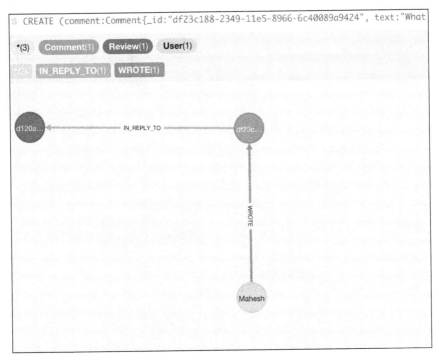

Figure 6.6: Adding comments to a review

To add a reply to an already existing comment, we can use the following query:

```
CREATE (new_comment:Comment{_id:"a3da3c5c-2350-11e5
   -9006-6c40089a9424", text: "Some issues with the
   air conditioner which led to a sleepless night",
   created_on: 1391723407.342643})
WITH new_comment
MATCH (comment:Comment{_id:"df23c188-2349-11e5-8966-
   6c40089a9424"}), (user:User{email:
   "hale.orison@gmail.com"})
MERGE (user)-[:WROTE]->(new_comment)-[:IN_REPLY_TO]->(comment)
RETURN user, new_comment, comment
```

The output of the preceding query is as follows:

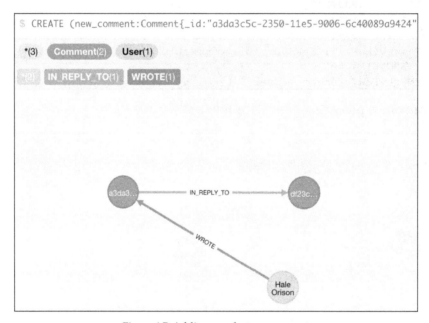

Figure 6.7: Adding a reply to a comment

We can add more comments to the review in the same way as we added the first one:

```
CREATE (comment:Comment{_id:"1e0a80de-2353-11e5-86b5-
   6c40089a942", text:"Thanks for updating this.",
   created_on:1390686607.342643})
WITH comment
MATCH (review:Review{_id:"d120a06e-2331-11e5-
   bf11-6c40089a9424"}), (user:User{email:
   "elijah.b@gmail.com"})
WITH review, user, comment
```

```
MERGE (review)<-[:IN_REPLY_TO]-(comment)
  <-[:WROTE]-(user)
RETURN review, comment, user
```

The output of the preceding query is as follows:

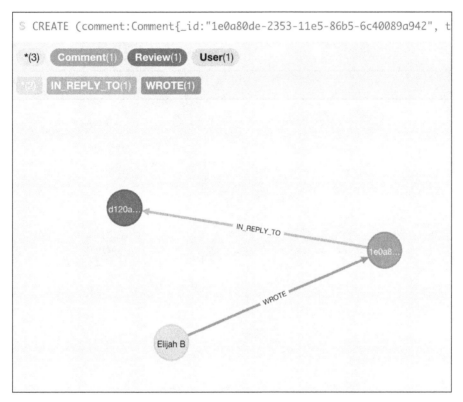

Figure 6.8: Adding additional comment to the review

To fetch the review along with its comments, we can use the following query:

```
MATCH p = (review:Review{_id:"d120a06e-2331-
  11e5-bf11-6c40089a9424"})<-[:IN_REPLY_TO*1..]-
  (comment:Comment)<-[:WROTE]-(user:User)
RETURN p
```

The output of the preceding query is as follows:

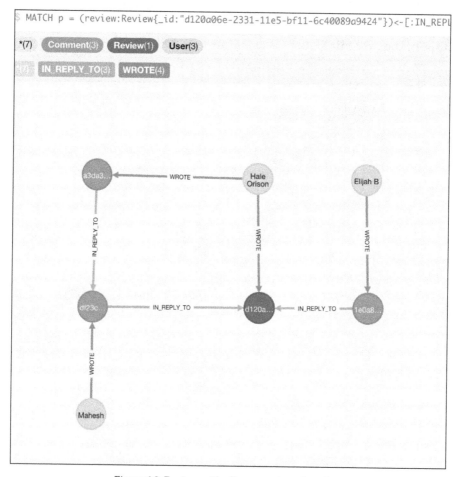

Figure 6.9: Review with all comments and replies

Considerations for modeling temporal data as chains

There are advantages to modeling temporal data as chains. The following points should be considered before modeling any data as a chain:

- Data should be modeled as a chain when the temporal relationship between them is important from a semantic perspective. Any communication with a request-response structure (for example, comments and e-mails) is suited to be modeled as a chain. Modeling the communication as a chain maintains the order in which the communication enters the system.

- In certain cases, there might be an implicit order in the data. For example, a visa application might go through multiple stages, which are in a particular order. Modeling these stages as chains would make sense.

- In certain cases, there might be a preferred order in which to present data. For example, most recent reviews make more sense, and hence the default for fetching reviews might be in reverse chronological order of the date of the stay. To optimize for the default scenario, we can model the data as a chain so that data can be fetched faster.

If the data doesn't fit into any of the categories mentioned in the previous bullets, then the data might not be suited to be modeled as a chain.

However, modeling data in chains has some downsides:

- Modeling the data as a chain will make it efficient for retrieval in a particular order, but might have performance penalties if the retrieval pattern needs to change

- Writing data to a chain that is ordered in reverse chronological order requires a complex query

Summary

In this chapter, we discussed modeling reviews and comments. We modeled comments as chains in order to maintain the semantic relationship between comments and replies. We discussed various queries that can be used to retrieve reviews and aggregation based on ratings. We also discussed the factors to be considered when deciding on modeling data as a chain.

In the next chapter, we will look at how we can model access control and construct queries that take into consideration the access control settings.

7
Modeling Access Control

In the previous chapters, we designed the database for an application that allows travelers to search for routes, view flights and hotels, check reviews for hotels, comment on reviews, and book flights. When multiple hotel chains operate using the same application (such as the one we are building), it helps if the hotel chains have access to modify the content that they wish to expose to the outside world.

In this chapter, we will explore:

- Creating access control structures in a graph
- Using access control structures to query and get selected data

Controlling access for content change

A hotel chain can have multiple hotels in different locations across cities or even countries, and each of these needs to edit its content. Employees of a hotel chain can be associated with particular hotels or regions. Assuming each hotel has autonomy in deciding and modifying their own content, we have the following scenarios to be addressed:

- Employees of a hotel chain should have access to modify the content for the hotels they have access to, depending on the access groups they are in
- Employees of a hotel shouldn't have access to modify any other hotel's content irrespective of the fact that there might be other hotels belonging to the same parent hotel chain
- Employees of a hotel chain shouldn't be able to access content of other hotel chains

Modeling hierarchies

To model employees and access control groups, we need to first modify our existing data to account for hierarchies in regions, countries, and cities. We also need to add hotel chains and their hierarchies. We can then apply the same practices used in modeling hierarchies to model access groups.

Modeling geographical regions

We already have airports and cities, which are geographical entities. We can add a couple of other entities such as country and region.

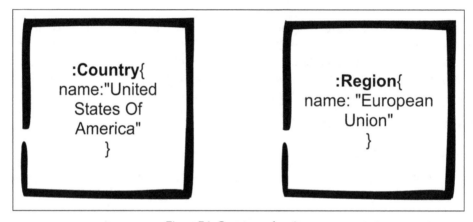

Figure 7.1: Country and region

A country or a region is uniquely identified by its name.

We can represent the relationship between airports, cities, countries, and regions in the following way:

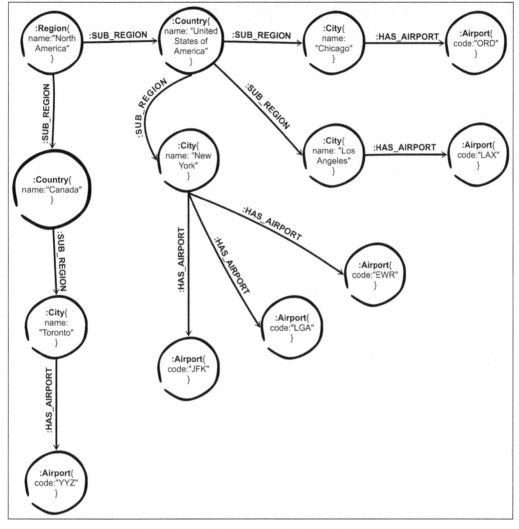

Figure 7.2: Regions, countries, cities, and airports

 The previous diagram representing *Regions, countries, cities, and airports* can be generalized to represent a hierarchy in Neo4j.

Adding countries and regions to Neo4j

We can add a constraint to ensure the uniqueness of a name across countries, shown as follows:

```
neo4j-sh (?)$ CREATE CONSTRAINT ON (country:Country)
  ASSERT country.name IS UNIQUE;
```

The output of the preceding query is as follows:

```
+-------------------+
| No data returned. |
+-------------------+
Constraints added: 1
```

To extract countries from cities, and connect cities to their respective countries, we can use the following query:

```
MATCH (city:City)
WITH city
MERGE (country:Country{name: city.country})
WITH country, city
MERGE (country)-[:SUB_REGION]->(city)
RETURN city, country
```

The output of the preceding query is as follows:

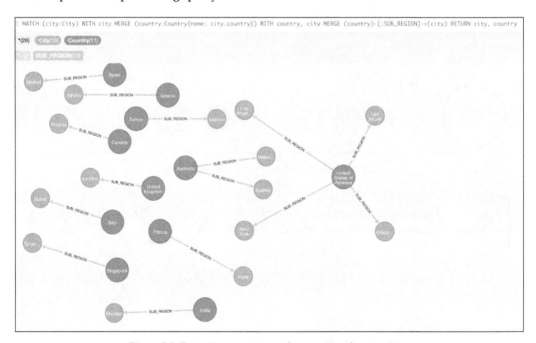

Figure 7.3: Extracting countries and connecting them to cities

We should also add a constraint on region names being unique as shown:

```
neo4j-sh (?)$ CREATE CONSTRAINT ON (region:Region)
  ASSERT region.name IS UNIQUE;
```

The output of the preceding query is as follows:

```
+-------------------+
| No data returned. |
+-------------------+
Constraints added: 1
```

Now, we can add regions to our data model and connect them to the countries by creating a region hierarchy. The following query creates a region with the name North America and adds Canada and United States of America to the region as :SUB_REGION:

```
MATCH (city:City)
WITH city
MERGE (country:Country{name: city.country})
WITH country, city
MERGE (country)-[:SUB_REGION]->(city)
RETURN city, country
```

The output of the preceding query is as shown:

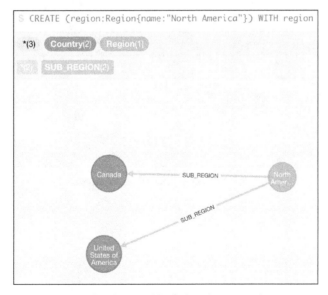

Figure 7.4: Creating North America as a region

We can add other regions to our data model using similar queries.

Add more regions using the `regions.cqy` file, which can be found with the code for this chapter.

The code can be downloaded from the publisher's website or from `https://github.com/maheshlal2910/neo4j_graph_data_modelling`.

The following query returns the whole region hierarchy along with the airports:

```
MATCH path = (region:Region)-[:SUB_REGION*1..]->
  (city:City)-[:HAS_AIRPORT]->(airport:Airport)
RETURN path
```

The output of the preceding query is as follows:

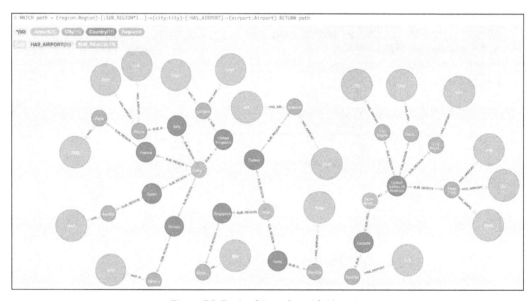

Figure 7.5: Region hierarchy with airports

In a more general sense, cities and countries can also be considered to be regions. We can add a label :Region to city and country nodes. The following query can be used for it:

```
neo4j-sh (?)$ MATCH (city:City), (country:Country)
   SET city :Region, country :Region;
```

The output of the preceding query is as shown:

```
+--------------------+
| No data returned.  |
+--------------------+
Labels added: 26
```

We can now proceed to the problem of modeling hotel chains, employees, and access control groups.

Modeling hotel chains

Hotel chains can be modeled as entities while hotels belong to chains.

Figure 7.6: Hotel chain

Hotel chains can be uniquely identified by their name. The relationship between hotels and chains can be depicted as shown in the following figure:

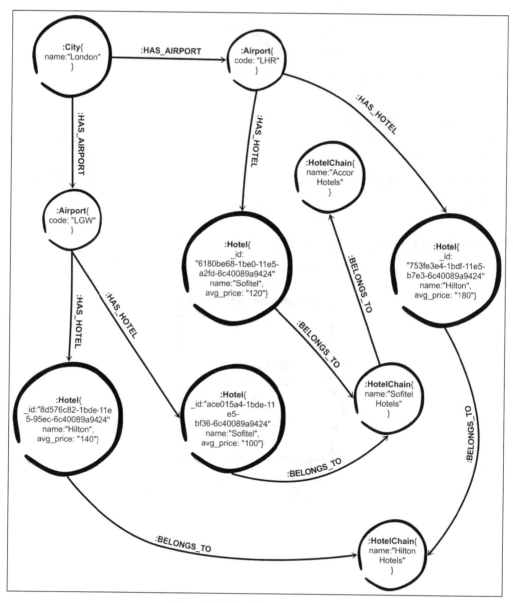

Figure 7.7: Hotel chains and hotels

Adding hotel chains to Neo4j

The following query adds a uniqueness constraint on the name of the hotel chain:

```
neo4j-sh (?)$ CREATE CONSTRAINT ON (chain:HotelChain)
   ASSERT chain.name IS UNIQUE;
```

The output of the preceding query is as follows:

```
+-------------------+
| No data returned. |
+-------------------+
Constraints added: 1
```

We can create a hotel chain and add hotels to that chain using the following query:

```
CREATE (chain:HotelChain{name:"Hilton Hotels"})
WITH chain
MATCH (hotel:Hotel) WHERE hotel.name IN ["Hilton", "Double Tree"]
MERGE (hotel)-[:BELONGS_TO]->(chain)
RETURN hotel, chain;
```

The output of the preceding query is as follows:

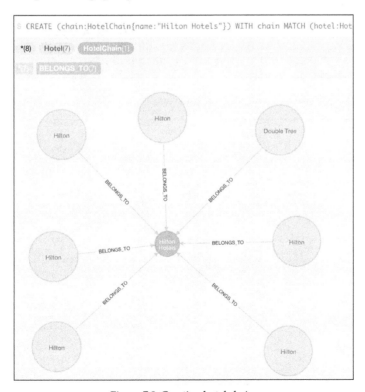

Figure 7.8: Creating hotel chains

Add more regions using `hotel_chains.cqy`, which can be found with the code for this chapter.

The code can be downloaded from the publisher's website or from `https://github.com/maheshlal2910/neo4j_graph_data_ modelling`.

The following query can be used to get the hierarchies of hotel chains, hotels, and regions:

```
MATCH p = (region:Region)-[:SUB_REGION*1..]->
  (city:City)-[:HAS_AIRPORT]->(airport:Airport)-
  [:HAS_HOTEL]->(hotel:Hotel)
WITH p, hotel
OPTIONAL MATCH (hotel:Hotel)-[:BELONGS_TO]-
  >(hotelChain:HotelChain)
RETURN
EXTRACT( node in FILTER(n in NODES(p)
  WHERE "Region" IN LABELS(n))| node.name) as region,
EXTRACT( node in FILTER(n in NODES(p) WHERE
  "Country" IN LABELS(n))| node.name) as country,
EXTRACT( node in FILTER(n in NODES(p) WHERE
  "City" IN LABELS(n))| node.name) as city,
EXTRACT( node in FILTER(n in NODES(p)
  WHERE "Airport" IN LABELS(n))| node.code) as airport,
EXTRACT( node in FILTER(n in NODES(p) WHERE
  "Hotel" IN LABELS(n))| node.name) as hotel,
hotelChain.name as chain;
```

The output of the preceding query is as follows:

region	country	city	airport	hotel	chain	parentChain
[North America]	[Canada]	[Toronto]	[YYZ]	[Four Points]	Sheraton Group	null
[North America]	[Canada]	[Toronto]	[YYZ]	[ALT Sheraton]	Sheraton Group	null
[North America]	[United States of America]	[New York]	[EWR]	[Wyndham]	Wyndham	null
[North America]	[United States of America]	[New York]	[LGA]	[LaGuardia Plaza]	Plaza Group	null
[North America]	[United States of America]	[New York]	[JFK]	[Hampton Inn]	Airport Inn Hospitality	null
[North America]	[United States of America]	[New York]	[JFK]	[Fairfield Inn]	Airport Inn Hospitality	null
[North America]	[United States of America]	[Los Angeles]	[LAX]	[LAX South Travelodge]	Travelodges	null
[North America]	[United States of America]	[Los Angeles]	[LAX]	[Sheraton]	Sheraton Group	null
[North America]	[United States of America]	[Los Angeles]	[LAX]	[Concourse]	Ambassador Suites	null
[North America]	[United States of America]	[Chicago]	[ORD]	[Embassy Suites]	Ambassador Suites	null
[North America]	[United States of America]	[Chicago]	[ORD]	[Hilton]	Hilton Hotels	null
[North America]	[United States of America]	[Chicago]	[ORD]	[Double Tree]	Hilton Hotels	null
[North America]	[United States of America]	[Las Vegas]	[LAS]	[Travelodge]	Travelodges	null
[North America]	[United States of America]	[Las Vegas]	[LAS]	[Hyatt]	Hyatt Group	null
[Asia]	[India]	[Mumbai]	[BOM]	[J W Marriot Sahar]	Marriot Group	null
[Asia]	[India]	[Mumbai]	[BOM]	[Hilton]	Hilton Hotels	null
[Asia]	[India]	[Mumbai]	[BOM]	[Ibis]	Ibis Hotels	Accor Hotels
[Asia]	[Singapore]	[Singapore]	[SIN]	[Ambassador]	Ambassador Suites	null
[Asia]	[Turkey]	[Istanbul]	[SAW]	[ISG]	ISG	null
[Asia]	[Turkey]	[Istanbul]	[IST]	[Radisson]	Radisson Group	null
[Asia]	[Turkey]	[Istanbul]	[IST]	[WOW]	Airavat Group	null
[European Union]	[United Kingdom]	[London]	[LHR]	[Yotel]	United Hotels	null
[European Union]	[United Kingdom]	[London]	[LHR]	[Sofitel]	Sofitel Hotels	Accor Hotels

Figure 7.9: Regions, countries, cities, airports, hotels, and chains

In a few cases such as `Sofitel`, `Mercure`, `Novotel`, and `Ibis`, there is a parent chain of each hotel chain.

Since region hierarchies and hotel chains have been added to the model, we can now add employees and permissions.

Modeling access control groups and employees

Access control requires that we define access groups and employees.

Figure 7.10: Employees and access groups

Access groups and employees can be identified uniquely by their _id properties. Both of these also have a property name.

Access groups are linked to a hotel chain and will define what region or location the access group has permission to access for writes. Access groups' levels and names will be different for different hotel chains.

Employees belong to a hotel chain and are associated with access groups. This association defines what they all have access to. The following diagram illustrates the relationship between hotels, hotel chains, access groups, and employees:

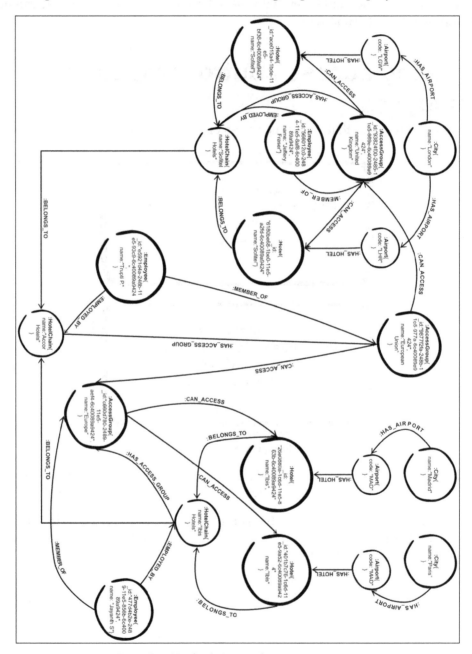

Figure 7.11: Hotels, chains, employees, access groups

Access groups can be named differently and have a different granularity for different chains. For example, **Ibis** hotels have an access group named **Europe**, which is applicable for all the countries in Europe, and thus, members of this group can access all hotels in Europe. **Sofitel** hotels, on the other hand, have a finer grained access group called **United Kingdom**, which allows access to hotels in the United Kingdom. The parent chain **Accor Hotels** has an access group named **European Union**, which has access to **Europe** and **United Kingdom**.

[For all further examples, we will add access groups to Accor hotels.]

Adding access groups to Neo4j

We can create a uniqueness constraint on the access group `_id` using the following query:

```
neo4j-sh (?)$ CREATE CONSTRAINT ON
    (accessGroup:AccessGroup) ASSERT accessGroup._id IS UNIQUE;
```

The output of the preceding query is as follows:

```
+-------------------+
| No data returned. |
+-------------------+
Constraints added: 1
```

To add an access group to a hotel chain for a particular region, we can use the following query:

```
MATCH (region:Region{name:"European Union"})-
    [:SUB_REGION*0..]->(:City)-[:HAS_AIRPORT]->
    (airport:Airport)-[:HAS_HOTEL]->(hotel:Hotel)-
    [:BELONGS_TO]->(chain:HotelChain{name:"Ibis Hotels"})
WITH hotel, chain
MERGE (accessGroup:AccessGroup{_id:"089cd024-
    249c-11e5-b902-6c40089a9424"}) ON CREATE SET
    accessGroup.name = "European Union"
WITH chain, hotel, accessGroup
CREATE UNIQUE (chain)-[:HAS_ACCESS_GROUP]->
    (accessGroup)-[:CAN_ACCESS]->(hotel)
RETURN chain, accessGroup, hotel
```

The output of the preceding query is as follows:

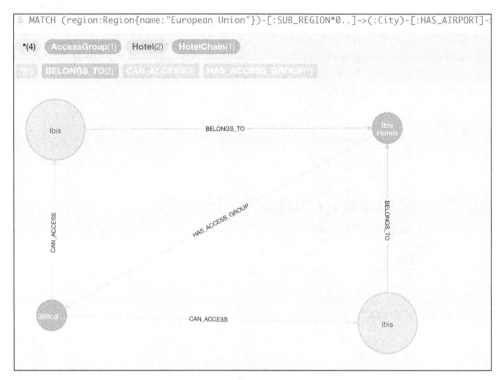

Figure 7.12: Adding access group to a region for a hotel chain

 Add more regions using `accor_subsidiary_hotels_access_groups.cqy` that can be found with the code for this chapter. The code can be downloaded from the publisher's website or from `https://github.com/maheshlal2910/neo4j_graph_data_modelling`.

To add an access group that can access other access groups, we can use the following query:

```
MATCH (subsidiaryAccessGroup:AccessGroup),
    (chain:HotelChain{name:"Accor Hotels"})
WHERE subsidiaryAccessGroup._id IN ["7506082e-24a2-
    11e5-b62b-6c40089a9424","539487e2-24a2-11e5-bb1b-
    6c40089a9424","cef89d02-24a1-11e5-821c-6c40089a9424",
    "089cd024-249c-11e5-b902-6c40089a9424"]
WITH subsidiaryAccessGroup, chain
MERGE (accessGroup:AccessGroup{_id:"57096838-24a3-
    11e5-87db-6c40089a9424"}) ON CREATE SET
    accessGroup.name = "European Union"
WITH subsidiaryAccessGroup, accessGroup, chain
CREATE UNIQUE (chain)-[:HAS_ACCESS_GROUP]->
    (accessGroup)-[:CAN_ACCESS]->(subsidiaryAccessGroup)
WITH chain, accessGroup
MATCH path = (chain)-[:HAS_ACCESS_GROUP]->
    (accessGroup)-[:CAN_ACCESS*1..]->(:Hotel)-
    [:BELONGS_TO]->(:HotelChain)
RETURN path
```

The output of the preceding query is as follows:

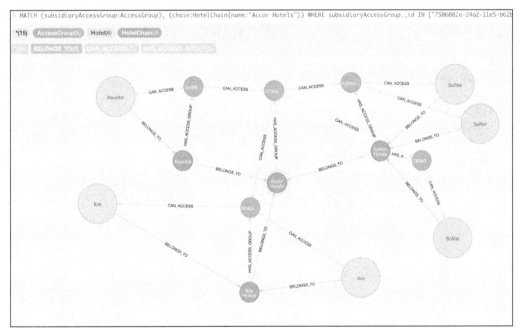

Figure 7.13: Adding access groups that can access other access groups

Add more regions using `accor_access_groups.cqy`, which can be found with the code for this chapter. The code can be downloaded from the publisher's website or from `https://github.com/maheshlal2910/neo4j_graph_data_modelling`.

Adding employees to Neo4j

We can add a constraint on the employee `_id` using the following query:

```
neo4j-sh (?)$ CREATE CONSTRAINT ON (emp:Employee)
    ASSERT emp._id IS UNIQUE;
```

The output of the preceding query is as follows:

```
+--------------------+
| No data returned.  |
+--------------------+
Constraints added: 1
```

The following query adds an employee to a hotel chain and assigns the employee to an access group:

```
MATCH (chain:HotelChain{name:"Accor Hotels"}),
    (euAccess:AccessGroup{_id:"57096838-24a3-
    11e5-87db-6c40089a9424"})
WITH chain, euAccess
MERGE (employee:Employee{_id:17812}) ON CREATE
    SET employee.name = "Jeoffery Fraser"
WITH employee, chain, euAccess
CREATE UNIQUE (chain)<-[:EMPLOYED_BY]-(employee)
    -[:MEMBER_OF]->(euAccess)
RETURN employee, euAccess, chain
```

The output of the preceding query is as follows:

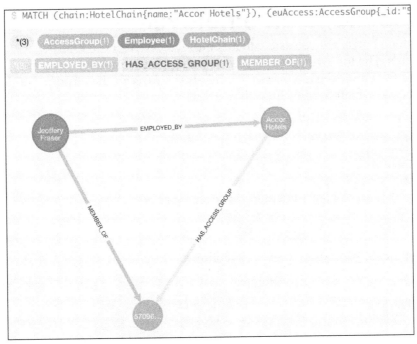

Figure 7.14: Adding an employee to a hotel chain and assigning the employee to a group

Add more regions using `employees.cqy` that can be found with the code for this chapter. The code can be downloaded from the publisher's website or from `https://github.com/maheshlal2910/neo4j_graph_data_modelling`.

Querying the data model to find what is accessible to an employee

To find which hotels are accessible to an employee, we can traverse the `:CAN_ACCESS` relationships. The following query gets all the hotels accessible to an employee via all the groups the employee has access to, and also returns all the airports and locations of the hotels to which the employee has access:

```
MATCH p = (chain:HotelChain)<-[:EMPLOYED_BY]-
   (employee:Employee{_id:17812})-[:MEMBER_OF]->
   (:AccessGroup)-[:CAN_ACCESS*0..]->(hotel:Hotel)-
   [:BELONGS_TO]->(hotelChain:HotelChain)
WITH p, hotel
MATCH (hotel)<-[:HAS_HOTEL]-(airport:Airport)<-
   [:HAS_AIRPORT]-(city:City)
RETURN p, hotel, airport, city
```

The output of the preceding query is as follows:

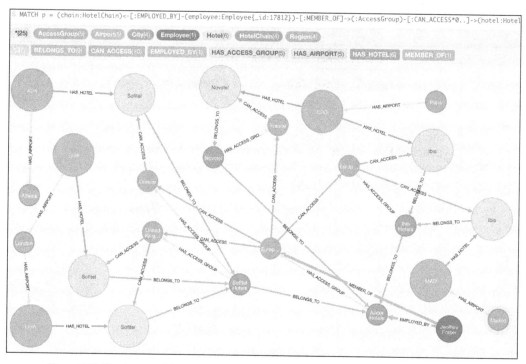

Figure 7.15: Hotels accessible to members of the European Union access group of Accor hotels

For an employee of a subsidiary of Accor hotels, the accessible hotels will be a smaller subset. The following query tries finding all hotels accessible to a different employee in a different hotel chain:

```
MATCH p = (chain:HotelChain)<-[:EMPLOYED_BY]-
  (employee:Employee{_id:78641})-[:MEMBER_OF]->
  (:AccessGroup)-[:CAN_ACCESS*0..]->(hotel:Hotel)-
  [:BELONGS_TO]->(hotelChain:HotelChain)
WITH p, hotel
MATCH (hotel)<-[:HAS_HOTEL]-(airport:Airport)<-
  [:HAS_AIRPORT]-(city:City)
RETURN p, hotel, airport, city
```

The output of the preceding query is as follows:

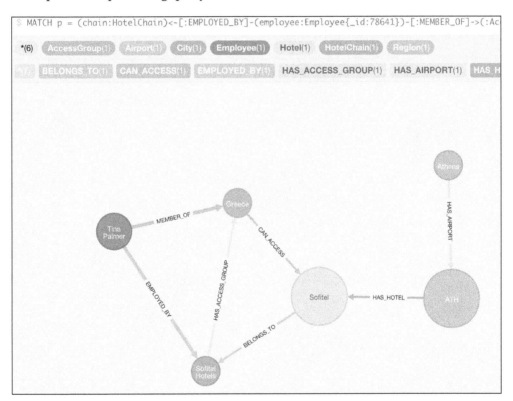

Figure 7.16: Hotels accessible to an employee of Sofitel who is member of the Greek access group

Summary

In this chapter, we explored how we can model access control in graphs. While we have created access groups according to the region, there might be different parameters on which we can create access groups. We also explored how to use the groups and accessible hotels to find which hotels are accessible to a particular employee.

In the next chapter, you will learn how to recommend hotels to travelers and analyzing data using Cypher.

8
Recommendations and Analysis of Historical Data

In the previous chapters, you learned how to use model flights and cities as a graph and have written queries to return flight routes. We also added airports, hotels, reviews for hotels, and access groups that we could use to decide which access rights an employee has.

In this chapter, we will explore how we can run recommendations using the data we have, and also see if we can uncover some patterns using historical data.

Recommending cities to travelers

We know which cities the travelers have traveled to on the basis of the journeys they have been a part of. This allows us to make recommendations to a traveler as to where they could travel next. Using information about where a user has traveled, and some information about the city, we can recommend better. There are multiple pieces of information of the place can be added, one of them being the category or the type of city.

We can consider cities as belonging to one or more of the following categories:

- **Streets**: This includes cities where there is rich street art, street food, and so on
- **Cosmopolitan hotspots**: This includes cities that are cosmopolitan
- **Romantic**: This includes cities which couples consider for a romantic holiday
- **Historical importance**: This includes cities with historical importance
- **Architecture**: This includes cities with beautiful architecture, both modern and classical
- **Business**: This includes cities that are business centers

These categories don't exist in our data and we will need to model them and associate them with cities.

Modeling categories

Categories can be modeled as nodes or labels. Modeling categories as labels is a simple approach. However, modeling categories as nodes is more flexible. A category modeled as a node allows us to represent hierarchies among categories, facilitates aggregation with ease, and also allows us to find the most relevant category using counts. While labels allow us to do aggregation, the resultant query will be difficult to understand. Modeling categories as nodes also allows us to add metadata to the category. The following figure suggests the model of a category node:

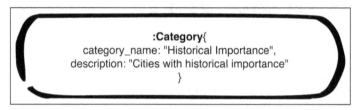

Figure 8.1: Category node

Categories have names and descriptions. They can be uniquely identified by their name. The following figure represents how a category will be related to a city:

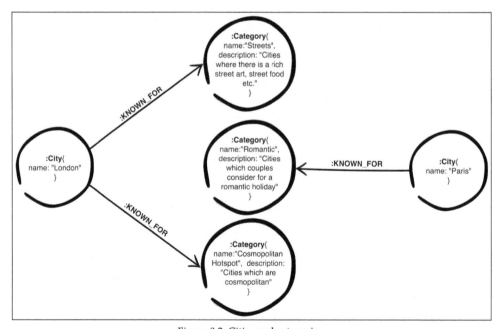

Figure 8.2: Cities and categories

A city can have multiple categories and will be connected to all categories that it has by a **:KNOWN_FOR** relationship.

Creating categories in Neo4j

We can create a constraint on the category name using the following query:

```
neo4j-sh (?)$ CREATE CONSTRAINT ON (c:Category)
   ASSERT c.name IS UNIQUE;
```

The output of the preceding query is as follows:

```
+-------------------+
| No data returned. |
+-------------------+
Constraints added: 1
```

Cities and categories

We can create a category using the following query:

```
CREATE (c:Category{name:"Streets",  description:
   "Cities where there is a rich street art
   , street food etc."}) RETURN c;
```

The output of the preceding query is as follows:

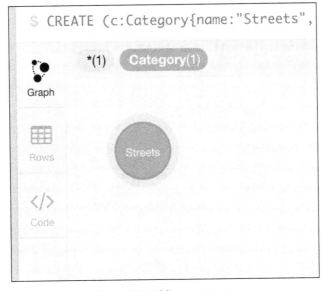

Figure 8.3: Adding a category

You can add more categories using the `categories.cqy` files, which can be found with the code for this chapter. The code can be downloaded from the publisher's website or from `https://github.com/maheshlal2910/neo4j_graph_data_modelling`.

Cities can have multiple categories associated with them, for example, Mumbai is known for business as well as historical importance. We can connect a city to a category using the following query:

```
neo4j-sh (?)$ MATCH (n:City{name:"Mumbai"}),
  (c:Category{name:"Cosmopolitan Hotspot"})
  CREATE UNIQUE (n)-[:KNOWN_FOR]->(c);
```

The output of the preceding query is as follows:

```
+--------------------+
| No data returned.  |
+--------------------+
Relationships created: 1
```

 You can connect more cities to categories using the `add_categories_to_cities.cqy` file that can be found with the code for this chapter. The code can be downloaded from the publisher's website or from `https://github.com/maheshlal2910/neo4j_graph_data_modelling`.

Recommending cities based on previous travels

A traveler might pass through multiple cities while travelling, however, we can't count each city as a "traveled" city. The traveler might just be transiting through some of the cities. The following query gives us information about all the cities the traveler has travelled to:

```
neo4j-sh (?)$ MATCH (passenger:Passenger
  {email:"vishal.p@gmail.com"})<-
  [:HAS_PASSENGER]-(b:Booking)-[:HAS_JOURNEY]->
  (:Journey)-[:BY_FLIGHT]->(:Flight)-[r]-
  (airport:Airport)
WITH DISTINCT b AS original_booking,
  COLLECT(airport) AS airports, passenger
```

```
WITH original_booking, FILTER(airport IN
  airports WHERE 1=LENGTH(FILTER
  (a IN airports WHERE a=airport)))
  AS distinct_airports, passenger
MATCH (airport:Airport)<-[:HAS_AIRPORT]-(city:City)
WHERE airport IN distinct_airports
RETURN  DISTINCT city.name;
```

The output of the preceding query is as follows:

```
+---------------+
| city.name     |
+---------------+
| "Los Angeles" |
| "London"      |
| "New York"    |
| "Mumbai"      |
+---------------+
4 rows
```

Using this information, we can now find out the categories that the traveler might be most interested in, and on the basis of the most common categories, we can recommend other cities satisfying those categories to travel to next. There might be categories that are of higher interest to a traveler, and we can use this information to find cities that the traveler might find more interesting. The following query calculates a travelers' category preferences and recommends cities that cover most of the categories:

```
MATCH (passenger:Passenger{email:
  "vishal.p@gmail.com"})<-[:HAS_PASSENGER]-
  (b:Booking)-[:HAS_JOURNEY]->(:Journey)-
  [:BY_FLIGHT]->(:Flight)-[r]-(airport:Airport)
WITH DISTINCT b AS original_booking, COLLECT(airport)
  AS airports, passenger
WITH original_booking, FILTER(airport IN airports WHERE
  1=LENGTH(FILTER(a IN airports WHERE a=airport)))
  AS distinct_airports, passenger
MATCH (airport:Airport)<-[:HAS_AIRPORT]-(city:City)
WHERE airport IN distinct_airports
WITH DISTINCT city
MATCH (city)-[:KNOWN_FOR]->(category:Category)
WITH DISTINCT category, COUNT(category) as relevance,
  COLLECT(city) as cities ORDER BY relevance DESC
MATCH (other_city:City)-[:KNOWN_FOR]->(category)
WHERE NOT other_city IN cities
```

```
RETURN DISTINCT other_city.name,
  COLLECT(category.name), COUNT(category.name)
  as relevance ORDER BY relevance DESC
```

The output of the preceding query is as follows:

other_city.name	COLLECT(category.name)	relevance
Madrid	[Business, Streets, Historical Importance]	3
Paris	[Business, Historical Importance]	2
Istanbul	[Streets, Historical Importance]	2
Melbourne	[Business, Streets]	2
Sydney	[Business, Streets]	2
Athens	[Business, Historical Importance]	2
Singapore	[Business, Cosmopolitan Hotspot]	2
Toronto	[Business]	1
Las Vegas	[Streets]	1
Chicago	[Business]	1
Rome	[Historical Importance]	1

Figure 8.4: Cities that might interest the traveler most

Recommending cities on the basis of other travelers

We can recommend cities to visit on the basis of other travelers as well. One of the simplest scenarios to consider is, if Alice and Bob have visited the same city, we can recommend other cities visited by Bob to Alice. The query is as follows:

```
neo4j-sh (?)$
//get all cities the traveller has been to
MATCH (passenger:Passenger{email:"vishal.p@gmail.com"})
  <-[:HAS_PASSENGER]-(b:Booking)-[:HAS_JOURNEY]->
  (:Journey)-[:BY_FLIGHT]->(:Flight)-[r]-(airport:Airport)
WITH DISTINCT b AS original_booking,
  COLLECT(airport) AS airports, passenger
WITH original_booking, FILTER(airport IN airports
  WHERE 1=LENGTH(FILTER(a IN airports WHERE
  a=airport))) AS distinct_airports, passenger
MATCH (airport:Airport)<-[:HAS_AIRPORT]-(city:City)
WHERE airport IN distinct_airports
WITH city, passenger
//fetch other passengers who have travelled to this city
MATCH (city)-[:HAS_AIRPORT]->(a:Airport)-[rel]-
  (:Flight)<-[:BY_FLIGHT]-(:Journey)<-[:HAS_JOURNEY]-
  (booking:Booking)-[:HAS_PASSENGER]->
  (other_passenger:Passenger)
```

```
WHERE other_passenger <> passenger
WITH DISTINCT other_passenger, city
//find all bookings of other passengers who have
  travelled to same city
MATCH (other_passenger)<-[:HAS_PASSENGER]-
  (other_booking:Booking)
WITH DISTINCT other_booking, city
//find all cities that the other traveller has
  visited and filter out the cities that have been already visited
MATCH (other_booking)-[:HAS_JOURNEY]->(j:Journey)-[:BY_FLIGHT]-
  >(:Flight)-[r]-(other_airport:Airport)
WITH DISTINCT other_booking._id as booking, COLLECT(DISTINCT
  j._id) as journey, COLLECT(other_airport)
  as other_airports, city
WITH FILTER(unique_airport IN other_airports WHERE
  1=LENGTH(FILTER(x IN other_airports
  WHERE x=unique_airport))) AS destination_airports,
  COLLECT(city) as visited
UNWIND destination_airports as airport
MATCH (airport:Airport)<-[:HAS_AIRPORT]-(other_city:City)
WHERE NOT other_city IN visited
RETURN DISTINCT other_city.name as recommended_cities;
```

The output of the preceding query is as follows:

```
+--------------------+
| recommended_cities |
+--------------------+
| "Singapore"        |
| "Melbourne"        |
+--------------------+
2 rows
```

There can be other variants of this recommendation where we recommend cities that Bob has visited and belong to categories that Alice is interested in. The possibilities for recommendations are bound by the data and how we can derive connections between them.

Recommending hotels to travelers

Reviews and ratings help travelers to decide on a hotel to stay at when travelling to or transiting through a particular place. However, reviews are dependent on people's personal tastes. A few other inputs that can help travelers make a better decision are:

- Hotels which are from the same chain

- Hotels which other similar travelers have stayed at

- Hotels in a particular price range

These parameters aren't well defined, and we will define each of these better when we explore each scenario. Also, these aren't the only parameters that necessarily need to be considered, as recommendations can be made around any set of parameters.

It's easier to start with recommending hotels from the same chain that the traveler has visited earlier. We will assume that a traveler has visited a hotel if he has written a review for it. In all the queries for the recommendation of a hotel, we have constrained the search to an airport since they are mostly transit hotels.

Recommending hotels from the same chains

In the following query, we search hotels at the Melbourne airport that belong to the same chain of hotels that the traveler has stayed at earlier:

```
neo4j-sh (?)$ MATCH (user:User{email:"mahesh.
  lal@gmail.com"})-[:WROTE]->(:Review)-[:FOR_HOTEL]-
  >(stayed:Hotel)-[:BELONGS_TO*1..]->(
chain:HotelChain)
WITH chain, stayed
MATCH (airport:Airport{code:"MEL"})-[:HAS_HOTEL]->
  (hotel:Hotel)-[:BELONGS_TO*1..]->(chain)
RETURN DISTINCT hotel.name as Hotel, COLLECT
  (DISTINCT chain.name) as Hotel_Groups,
  COLLECT(DISTINCT stayed.name) AS Previous_Stays ;
```

The output of the preceding query is as follows:

```
+----------------------------------------------------------------+
| Hotel  | Hotel_Groups                  | Previous_Stays        |
+----------------------------------------------------------------+
| "Ibis" | ["Ibis Hotels","Accor Hotels"] | ["Ibis","Sofitel"] |
+----------------------------------------------------------------+
1 row
```

Recommending hotels visited by similar travelers

The similarity of one traveler to another depends on multiple factors. We can say that the travelers who have stayed in the same hotels are similar. The following query recommends hotels in descending order of the number of similar travelers who have stayed at the hotel:

```
MATCH (user:User{email:"mahesh.lal@gmail.com"})-[:WROTE]-
  >(:Review)-[:FOR_HOTEL]->(stayed:Hotel)<-[:FOR_HOTEL]-
  (:Review)<-[:WROTE]-(other_traveller:User)
WHERE NOT other_traveller = user
WITH other_traveller
MATCH (other_traveller)-[:WROTE]->(:Review)-[:FOR_HOTEL]-
  >(hotel:Hotel)<-[:HAS_HOTEL]-(airport:Airport{code:"IST"})
RETURN
DISTINCT hotel.name as Hotel,
COLLECT(DISTINCT other_traveller.name) AS Similar_travellers,
COUNT (DISTINCT other_traveller) AS
  number_of_similar_travellers_who_stayed_here
ORDER BY number_of_similar_travellers_who_stayed_here DESC
```

The output of the preceding query is as follows:

Hotel	Similar_travellers	number_of_similar_travellers_who_stayed_here
Radisson	[Abet Ali, Shambhu Dayal, Sadique T, Dominique Shepard]	4
WOW	[Shambhu Dayal]	1

Figure 8.5: Recommended hotels based on similar people

We can also tweak the same query to recommend hotels based on an average rating given to them by similar travelers. Before we try the query, we should add overall_rating to each review, which is an average of ratings on all parameters within a review, as shown:

```
neo4j-sh (?)$ MATCH (review:Review)
SET review.overall_rating = toFloat
  (review.value_for_money + review.food +
  review.comfort + review.service)/4;
```

The output of the preceding query is as follows:

```
+-------------------+
| No data returned. |
+-------------------+
Properties set: 159
```

We can now write a query to recommend hotels based on average ratings by similar travelers:

```
MATCH (user:User{email:"mahesh.lal@gmail.com"})-
  [:WROTE]->(:Review)-[:FOR_HOTEL]->(stayed:Hotel)
  <-[:FOR_HOTEL]-(:Review)<-[:WROTE]-(other_traveller:User)
WHERE NOT other_traveller = user
WITH other_traveller
MATCH (other_traveller)-[:WROTE]->
  (r:Review)-[:FOR_HOTEL]->(hotel:Hotel)
  <-[:HAS_HOTEL]-(airport:Airport{code:"IST"})
RETURN
DISTINCT hotel.name as Hotel,
COLLECT(DISTINCT other_traveller.name)
  AS Similar_travellers,
SUM(r.overall_rating)/COUNT (DISTINCT
  other_traveller) AS avg_rating_by_similar_travellers
ORDER BY avg_rating_by_similar_travelers DESC
```

The output of the preceding query is as follows:

Hotel	Similar_travellers	avg_rating_by_similar_travellers
WOW	[Shambhu Dayal]	6
Radisson	[Abet Ali, Shambhu Dayal, Sadique T, Dominique Shepard]	5.875

Figure 8.6: Recommending hotels based on average rating by similar travelers

Recommending hotels that match a price range

Considering that a traveler has stayed at multiple places, we can find the max price of the hotels visited. Based on this price, we can even suggest cheaper hotels at a particular location, as shown:

```
MATCH (user:User{email:"brian.heritage@hotmail.com"})
  -[:WROTE]->(:Review)-[:FOR_HOTEL]->(hotel:Hotel)
WITH MAX(hotel.price) AS max_price
MATCH (airport:Airport{code:"ORD"})-[:HAS_HOTEL]
  ->(hotel:Hotel)
```

```
WHERE hotel.price <= max_price
RETURN hotel.name, hotel.price
```

The output of the preceding query is as follows:

hotel.name	hotel.price
Embassy Suites	130
Double Tree	150

Figure 8.7: Recommending hotels based maximum price paid for a hotel historically

Improving recommendations

Though we have relied on the data already present to recommend hotels, there are several other parameters that can be used to recommend hotels. Recommendations can be improved by capturing more data for the user and increasing the data captured about hotels, for example, age of the user, the star rating of a hotel, assigned categories to hotels, and so on.

Analysis of the historical data

We have explored how to use the data model to enable a traveler to find what they need. With this data and some clever querying, we can also discover some trends that can help the businesses. Given we have the year, month, and day of bookings and hotel stays, we can venture into analyzing data and behavior patterns of individuals, and how it affects the businesses (hotels and airlines).

Querying to discover patterns

Bookings are not spread across the year evenly. There will always be months when the number of bookings made far exceeds the number of bookings during other months. The following query gives the number of bookings made for each month:

```
neo4j-sh (?)$ MATCH (booking:Booking)
WITH COLLECT(booking) AS bookings, booking
RETURN DISTINCT booking.month AS month, COUNT(bookings)
  AS num_of_bookings
ORDER BY num_of_bookings DESC;
```

The output of the preceding query is as follows:

```
+-----------------------------+
| month | num_of_bookings |
+-----------------------------+
| 12    | 7               |
| 10    | 3               |
| 1     | 3               |
| 3     | 1               |
+-----------------------------+
4 rows
```

Bookings are generally made in advance, and journey dates are different from the booking dates. As a corollary, peak journey months might be different as compared to peak booking months. Information about this can help in planning out promotional offer schedules to attract more sales. The following query gives us insight into when people travel the most:

```
neo4j-sh (?)$ MATCH (journey:Journey)
WITH COLLECT(journey) AS journeys, journey
RETURN DISTINCT journey.month AS month, COUNT(journeys)
   AS num_of_journeys
ORDER BY num_of_journeys DESC;
```

The output of the preceding query is as follows:

```
+-----------------------------+
| month | num_of_journeys |
+-----------------------------+
| 1     | 7               |
| 3     | 3               |
| 11    | 2               |
| 5     | 2               |
| 4     | 1               |
+-----------------------------+
5 rows
```

Certain travelers travel in a particular season- or month-defined range of days. Having access to information about when a person is likely to travel can help in designing offers and personalized promotions. The following query fetches information about when a particular traveler travels:

```
neo4j-sh (?)$ MATCH (p1:Passenger{email:"mahesh.lal@gmail.com"})
   <-[:HAS_PASSENGER]-(:Booking)-[:HAS_JOURNEY]->
   (journey:Journey)
WITH COLLECT(journey) AS journeys, journey, p1
```

```
RETURN DISTINCT journey.month AS month, COUNT(journeys)
  AS count_journeys, p1.name as traveller_name
ORDER BY count_journeys DESC;
```

The output of the preceding query is as follows:

```
+--------------------------------------------+
| month | count_journeys | traveller_name   |
+--------------------------------------------+
| 1     | 4              | "Mahesh Lal"     |
| 11    | 2              | "Mahesh Lal"     |
| 5     | 1              | "Mahesh Lal"     |
| 4     | 1              | "Mahesh Lal"     |
+--------------------------------------------+
4 rows
```

Hotels get reviews throughout the year, and there are times when we might want to see how the average ratings of a hotel change in a year. The following query gives us an insight into how a hotel chain has been rated over the past three years:

```
MATCH (chain:HotelChain{name:"Hilton Hotels"})<-
  [:BELONGS_TO]-(hotel:Hotel)<-[:FOR_HOTEL]-(review:Review)
WITH review.stay_year as year, SUM(review.overall_rating) AS
  total_rating, COUNT(review) AS total_reviews,
  chain.name as group
RETURN DISTINCT year, SUM(total_rating/total_reviews)
  as avg_rating, total_rating, total_reviews, group
ORDER BY avg_rating DESC
```

The output of the preceding query is as follows:

year	avg_rating	total_rating	total_reviews	group
2015	2.75	8.25	3	Hilton Hotels
2014	2.638888888888889	47.5	18	Hilton Hotels
2013	2.272727272727273	25	11	Hilton Hotels

Figure 8.8: Average ratings of Hilton hotels over past 3 years

These are examples of a much larger set of analysis queries that can be run on the existing data.

ary

, you learned how to recommend hotels and cities to travel to using een stored in Neo4j. We also explored a few queries that analyzed and gave us some useful statistics. The next chapter guides you on ɔm here.

9
Wrapping Up

In the previous chapters, we saw examples of how to model various types of systems by taking examples of subsystems of a travel booking application. Taking a relatively straightforward graph problem, we expanded the problem statement and plotted more information on the graph. We explored the details of how to model certain systems and discussed design decisions. While we have covered a wide variety of designs decisions that can be adopted for different scenarios, the examples covered are by no means exhaustive. For example, we can enhance the user experience by adding location-based features for the travelers, and we can build more information into the Bookings subgraph by allowing for sequencing among the journeys of a booking.

There is no correct model

Modeling is a balancing act between the present and the future. It is important to understand that a data model is never perfect for all the problems that we might try to solve. We make compromises on certain parameters, while optimizing for others. Given more information and insight into the future of the business, the current model might feel inadequate. This is not an exception, and should be expected. Redesigning and data remodeling is a process that repeats itself multiple times over a product's life cycle.

Further reading and exploration

Graphs are being widely used in multiple domains, including, but not limited to, medical research, transportation, auditing, and financial risk analysis. For finding out more about modeling, the Neo4j mailing list on Google Groups is a good place. Occasionally, there are interesting modeling problems that people get down to solving. Alternately, a showcase of which problems people are solving using graphs in general and Neo4j in particular can be found at http://gist.neo4j.org/. For more use cases where Neo4j has been used, http://neo4j.com/use-cases/ is a good resource. Following @neo4j on Twitter is a good way to keep up with the happenings in the Neo4j world.

What to watch out for while using Neo4j

While Neo4j is a really handy tool and graphs are a good way to represent data, they are not suited for every single problem that is out there. There are definitely good cases where we can use an RDBMS more effectively. For example, if the application's main task is to aggregate and crunch on data that fits into a single table, then RDBMS is a better option. For other cases such as profiles and user preferences, it makes more sense to store them in a DocStore. Also, large documents are not meant to be stored in Neo4j. For full-text querying apart from querying based on field/label, Neo4j might only be a part of the solution; something such as Solr or Elasticsearch should be used along with Neo4j to get the full-text search working at scale. Caching is best left to solutions such as memcached. While graphs are a great tool, overusing them and trying to fit a non-graph use case into a graph will more often than not result in failure or at least the cost of maintenance will be prohibitively high.

Another limitation of Neo4j (more of a limitation of graphs than Neo4j), as with all native graph stores, is that it can't be sharded across machines. If we discover that the graph is going to increase beyond a certain size on the disk, or exceed the limits on numbers of nodes and relationships (32 billion nodes and 65 billion relationships), we should think of ways of restructuring the data in the graph so that it helps in sharding. A few practices that can help when we have to eventually partition the database are:

- Identifying relationships that can be turned to properties. If done well and indexed, the properties can act as implicit relationships. This reduces the interconnectedness of a graph, allowing us to partition it. Supernodes are candidates for conversion to properties. They are nodes to which hundreds, thousands or millions of other nodes are linked by relationships.

- If the problem domain is a large and complex interaction of multiple subdomains and is difficult to fit into one graph, modeling each of these domains in a separate graph might be beneficial. Relationships across subdomains can be represented by properties.

If we keep these caveats in mind while designing our graph data models, we can go a long way before hitting performance and other engineering issues.

Index

Thank you for buying
Neo4j Graph Data Modeling

About Packt Publishing

Packt, pronounced 'packed', published its first book, *Mastering phpMyAdmin for Effective MySQL Management*, in April 2004, and subsequently continued to specialize in publishing highly focused books on specific technologies and solutions.

Our books and publications share the experiences of your fellow IT professionals in adapting and customizing today's systems, applications, and frameworks. Our solution-based books give you the knowledge and power to customize the software and technologies you're using to get the job done. Packt books are more specific and less general than the IT books you have seen in the past. Our unique business model allows us to bring you more focused information, giving you more of what you need to know, and less of what you don't.

Packt is a modern yet unique publishing company that focuses on producing quality, cutting-edge books for communities of developers, administrators, and newbies alike. For more information, please visit our website at www.packtpub.com.

About Packt Open Source

In 2010, Packt launched two new brands, Packt Open Source and Packt Enterprise, in order to continue its focus on specialization. This book is part of the Packt Open Source brand, home to books published on software built around open source licenses, and offering information to anybody from advanced developers to budding web designers. The Open Source brand also runs Packt's Open Source Royalty Scheme, by which Packt gives a royalty to each open source project about whose software a book is sold.

Writing for Packt

We welcome all inquiries from people who are interested in authoring. Book proposals should be sent to author@packtpub.com. If your book idea is still at an early stage and you would like to discuss it first before writing a formal book proposal, then please contact us; one of our commissioning editors will get in touch with you.

We're not just looking for published authors; if you have strong technical skills but no writing experience, our experienced editors can help you develop a writing career, or simply get some additional reward for your expertise.

Learning Neo4j

ISBN: 978-1-84951-716-4   Paperback: 222 pages

Run blazingly fast queries on complex graph datasets with the power of the Neo4j graph database

1. Get acquainted with graph database systems and apply them in real-world use cases.

2. Get started with Neo4j, a unique NOSQL database system that focuses on tackling data complexity.

3. A practical guide filled with sample queries, installation procedures, and useful pointers to other information sources.

Neo4j Essentials

ISBN: 978-1-78355-517-8   Paperback: 200 pages

Leverage the power of Neo4j to design, implement, and deliver top-notch projects

1. Understand, in detail, the Pattern matching theory, and cypher optimization.

2. Use Neo4j models combined with the power of Cypher to sketch and start working quickly.

3. A fast-paced, example-oriented guide to help you integrate Neo4j in standard Java applications.

Please check **www.PacktPub.com** for information on our titles

Network Graph Analysis and Visualization with Gephi

ISBN: 978-1-78328-013-1   Paperback: 116 pages

Visualize and analyze your data swiftly using dynamic network graphs built with Gephi

1. Use your own data to create network graphs displaying complex relationships between several types of data elements.

2. Learn about nodes and edges, and customize your graphs using size, color, and weight attributes.

3. Filter your graphs to focus on the key information you need to see and publish your network graphs to the Web.

Data Visualization: a successful design process

ISBN: 978-1-84969-346-2   Paperback: 206 pages

A structured design approach to equip you with the knowledge of how to successfully accomplish any data visualization challenge efficiently and effectively

1. A portable, versatile and flexible data visualization design approach that will help you navigate the complex path towards success.

2. Explains the many different reasons for creating visualizations and identifies the key parameters which lead to very different design options.

3. Thorough explanation of the many visual variables and visualization taxonomy to provide you with a menu of creative options.

CPSIA information can be obtained
at www.ICGtesting.com
Printed in the USA
BVHW071031050120
568585BV00011B/670/P